CONSCIOUS PARENTING
OF YOUR TODDLER

CONSCIOUS PARENTING
of Your Toddler

Strategies to Turn Discipline into Growth and Connection

MIHAELA PLUGARASU, MS

Illustrations by Irena Freitas

ROCKRIDGE
PRESS

Interior and Cover Designer: Heather Krakora
Art Producer: Tom Hood
Editor: Sabrina Young
Production Editor: Ruth Sakata Corley

Illustrations ©2020 Irena Freitas

ISBN: Print 978-1-64739-667-1 | eBook 978-1-64739-391-5

R0

***Dedicated to** my son, Alexander.*
You are the spiritual teacher
I needed to awaken.
I am grateful for you being you.
I am grateful you chose me
to be your mom. Keep shining
your light, my son. Thank you
for teaching me every day
what it means to be authentic,
brave, and vulnerable.
Thank you for teaching me
the beauty of "now" in play
and laughter. Thank you for
teaching me to love unconditionally.
I love you always.

CONTENTS

Your children are not your children.
They are the sons and daughters of
Life's longing for itself.
They come through you but
not from you,
And though they are with you
yet they belong not to you.
You may give them your love
but not your thoughts,
For they have their own thoughts.
You may house their bodies
but not their souls,
For their souls dwell in
the house of tomorrow,
which you cannot visit,
not even in your dreams.
You may strive to be like them,
but seek not to make them like you.

"On Children," Kahlil Gibran (1883–1931)

INTRODUCTION

To all the parents who are excited about conscious parenting, welcome! Thank you for joining me in this journey.

I am a mom, co-parent, college instructor, and certified parent educator. I became a licensed elementary school teacher at only 18 years old, and I have been around young children all my life, either as a teacher or a caretaker. However, it was not until I became a mother that I felt the immense responsibility I had toward my child: to ensure that he is growing up in an emotionally safe environment to express his feelings, needs, and wants, so he can become the authentic individual he was born to be. I wanted to be there for him, fully present, mindful, and resourceful, as all new parents do. Yet I was failing and I didn't know why. Fortunately, I quickly realized that I needed to make profound changes within myself. I realized that my own lack of self-awareness was preventing me from being the mother I wanted to be. Since then, I've embarked on the most beautiful journey of all: to meet myself for the first time every day.

I committed to the work of self-growth and self-awareness. I started asking myself these questions:

- ▸ Who am I really?
- ▸ Why do I behave this way right now?
- ▸ What am I afraid of?
- ▸ Why do I feel emotionally paralyzed in certain moments and not others?

I am now a parenting-by-connection certified parent instructor. I have had the privilege and joy of working with diverse groups of parents in workshops and parent support groups.

Children are born whole. We are in perfect symbiosis during pregnancy and cannot wait to meet them for the first time. When they come to us, they are the embodiment of love and long to belong. They look at us with untouched innocence and trust. We look at their beautiful tiny faces and we melt.

Then we quickly discover that parenting is hard, exhausting, and often isolating. We become aware of feelings, reactions, and thoughts that we never knew existed inside of us. Often, we feel powerless, guilty, and ashamed of our own behaviors.

Conscious parenting is about the relationship we have with ourselves. This is a courageous act because it challenges our beliefs about success, well-being, happiness, authority, autonomy, self-sacrifice, social status, responsibility, and unconditional love. As you embark on this journey, I invite you to keep this "ABC" in mind as pillars of conscious parenting: (self)-Awareness, Be(-ing) Present, and Connection.

It will all make sense in the end, I promise.

Yours in gratitude and growth,
Mihaela

Part One

PRINCIPLES OF CONSCIOUS PARENTING

This book is divided into two parts. Part One will introduce you to the principles of conscious parenting and give you an in-depth explanation of what each one entails. Please take the time to review this section often.

GETTING STARTED WITH CONSCIOUS PARENTING

This chapter will introduce you to the key ideas behind conscious parenting. These ideas will help you learn to connect more with your inner self, trust yourself, and rely on that inner voice and guidance during parenting moments that feel difficult and challenging with your toddler.

Conscious parenting is a process of self-reflection, honesty, and the uprooting of limiting, harmful beliefs. We do this work in order to avoid passing these beliefs on to our children. This process is a lifelong journey—we don't know where it will take us, and it has no finish line. We might become discouraged by the pain or the time it takes, but as long as we stay committed, we remain on the right path.

This is the bravery of conscious parenting—it's an approach that requires dedication, commitment, strength, and patience. The reward is harmony, awareness, and emotional connection with your child.

WHAT IS CONSCIOUS PARENTING?

Conscious parenting is a relationship-based process in which parents look inward and choose to expand their self-awareness and leadership with the inevitable results of connection, authenticity, and personal evolution for both the child and the parent.

Conscious parenting is not about being perfect (perfection in parenting simply doesn't exist) or having all the right answers all the time. It's about looking inward and finding the answers within you. Thus, conscious parenting is self-parenting.

The Key Ideas of Conscious Parenting

Conscious parenting, or self-parenting, is not a new concept. It is based on the understanding that adults raised in unhealthy family environments may risk passing on learned negative behaviors to their children once they become parents. If we as children did not have our emotional needs met for safety, connection, and protection, our survival instinct may have created necessary self-defense mechanisms to keep us secure. If we were exposed to the same type of painful or traumatic experiences over and over again in our childhoods, these self-defense mechanisms become ingrained beliefs that we carry on into adulthood.

My child is the mirror I need to heal. I am in my power when I choose to connect instead of react.

You and your child mirror each other. By reflecting us back to ourselves, our kids reveal the unresolved and unintegrated childhood wounds that we need to heal. If we are unaware of the emotional baggage we bring into the parent-child relationship, we risk passing on the same pain, hurt, and wounds, like a generational curse.

Emotional connection is key to preventing this from happening. In fact, it takes priority over disciplining or correcting a child's behavior. While protecting and restoring the emotional connection in difficult parenting moments is not easy, if a parent becomes aware of their own emotional inner state first, they can then find the strength to separate their emotions from those of their child in order to meet the little one's needs first.

How do we, as parents, support this emotional connection? By following these five practical steps:

1. Find calm in the heat of the moment

2. Understand your toddler's behavior

3. Establish a feeling of safety

4. Connect emotionally

5. Learn to stay connected

The key idea behind conscious parenting is that our responsibility is to ourselves first in order to be the parents we want to be. These responsibilities include the following:

- Investigating the hurt brought to the surface, from the unconscious to the conscious awareness.
- Integrating those experiences in a way that we can learn from.
- Embracing our own evolution as we heal.

We are not bad parents, only hurt and fragmented adults. When these old childhood wounds show up in our parenting, they appear as fears, conscious or unconscious. However, fears are not all equal and not always easy to detect.

Other Parenting Approaches

Parenting is a learning process, and it's important to find the approach that works for you. Becoming knowledgeable about, and experimenting with, other approaches that are similar to conscious parenting is part of educating yourself on how to be a better parent. All knowledge will eventually culminate into your own self-leadership and parenting.

There are several parenting approaches that are popular today, and many share core values with the principles of conscious parenting.

ATTACHMENT PARENTING

Rooted in attachment theory, this method of parenting places emphasis on the parent-child bond prior to birth. An "attached parent" nurtures this bond after pregnancy and into the first years of the child's life.

Attachment Parenting International, a not-for-profit advocacy organization for attachment parenting worldwide, promotes eight parenting principles, including providing consistent and caring love, practicing positive discipline, and striving for balance in your personal and family life.

AUTHENTIC PARENTING

This parenting approach shares common values with conscious parenting, teaching parents that when children are praised for their behaviors, or when the outcomes of their actions are labeled (good and bad), they lose their inner authenticity. Naomi Aldort, the author of *Raising Our Children, Raising Ourselves*, teaches the "SALVE" formula to solve conflicts and stop training children to seek approval from parents:

Self-talk (separate yourself from your child's behavior)

Attention on the child

Listen

Validate

Empower the child (instead of trying to fix them or the situation)

AWARE PARENTING

Aware parenting was developed by Aletha Solter, PhD, a respected developmental psychologist who studied with the renowned psychologist Jean Piaget at the University of Geneva in Switzerland. Similar to authentic parenting and attachment parenting, aware parenting focuses on paying attention to a child's need in the moment, not the behavior.

In her first book, *The Aware Baby,* and four others that followed, Dr. Solter promotes three guiding aspects of aware parenting:

1. Attachment-style parenting

2. Nonpunitive discipline

3. Healing from stress and trauma

These aspects teach parents to accept the full range of a child's emotions, set firm but loving limits, and accept and acknowledge a child's development while honoring their own needs and emotions as parents.

POSITIVE PARENTING WITH POSITIVE DISCIPLINE

Founded by Jane Nelsen, EdD, and based on the work of the late Viennese psychiatrists Alfred Adler and Rudolf Dreikurs, positive parenting promotes positive discipline at home and at school. It is meant to teach and cannot be punitive or permissive. There are five criteria for positive discipline:

1. Kindness and firmness are necessary at the same time.

2. Children have an innate need for belonging and significance.

3. It focuses on long-term effectiveness.

4. It teaches social and life skills, such as problem solving, empathy, and collaboration.

5. It shows kids they are capable and have personal power and autonomy.

Positive parenting teaches how to set kind but firm limits, while allowing a child to satisfy their natural need for exploration and self-development.

PARENTING BY CONNECTION

This approach promotes connection in the parent-child relationship through five listening tools. It was developed by Patty Wipfler, the founder of Hand in Hand Parenting, a not-for-profit organization in Palo Alto, California. Parenting by connection teaches parents how to handle difficult situations by listening to and allowing a little one's hurt feelings to be expressed and healed, and providing a safe and loving presence.

Four of the five listening tools are parent-to-child oriented:

1. Special time

2. Staylistening

3. Setting limits

4. Playlistening

The fifth tool, listening partnership, is parent-to-parent oriented. It recognizes that parents need (and deserve) mutual support in order to listen to their children.

WHAT MAKES CONSCIOUS PARENTING DIFFERENT?

Conscious parenting is different because it is about the relationship we have with ourselves. When we understand our unresolved pain and fears, rather than reacting, we can train our mind to discover the unconscious beliefs and unresolved hurts that have been triggered.

When we react, it is usually dictated by conscious or unconscious fear. This emotion shows up in many ways. We might feel afraid and have the following thoughts:

- "I want the best for my child."
- "I want my child to be happy."
- "I would do anything to make sure my child has a good start in life."
- "I do this because I love my child."

- "I know what's best for my toddler because she is too young."
- "I didn't have a happy childhood and I don't want my child to experience that."

While these thoughts seem justified and logical, they all point to one ugly truth: Parents unconsciously use the relationship with their child to meet their unsatisfied needs for self-realization, approval, or control. That need for control or approval activates our fear state, and when we act out from that place, we cannot be in our hearts.

Fear and love cannot coexist simultaneously. If we are unaware when we act out of fear, we pass on our wounds to our child. Conscious parenting helps us become aware of our fear and need for control so that we can choose instead to heal our past and open our hearts. Our little one offers an opportunity to practice this self-awareness, which makes the healing process equally painful *and* miraculous.

Using Conflicts to Teach Skills

Conflict when parenting is inevitable. We tell our child to do one thing and they do the opposite. We cook a healthy meal and they refuse to eat. We decide it's bedtime and they still want to play. We've all been there, and it's easy to quickly lose our patience.

Here's an example: One morning, I was late for work and my preschool-age son refused to leave his room. He was crying and upset because he couldn't find a particular toy and he wouldn't go to school without it. I tried to stay calm and even helped him search for the toy, but eventually I lost my patience and yelled. In that moment, I lost my mind: I became scary and unloving.

He eventually came with me and after I dropped him off at daycare, I started to cry. I felt so guilty and ashamed. I understood the negative effects of yelling at my child, but I still acted against my values of unconditional love and emotional connection. That day, I looked close within myself and I recognized the old wounds that were calling for attention:

- Lack of clear personal boundaries
- Lack of preventive self-care
- Feeling unseen and unworthy of receiving love from those around me
- Feeling unsafe
- Feeling others' lack of empathy toward me
- Feeling incapable

Now that I recognize these wounds, I see how I could have used this conflict to teach my toddler better skills and model appropriate behavior. Rather than yelling, I could have walked away for a few minutes to calm down and come back to the present moment.

Importance of Modeling Appropriate Behaviors

Children can feel our energy. They pick up on nonverbal cues such as tone of voice, facial expressions, and physical closeness. When we mess up (such as when we yell), we must repair the broken emotional connection. Apologizing to your toddler sets the stage for a future relationship based on mutual respect and emotional safety. It gives your child a reference point and an appropriate behavior to model.

HOW TO MODEL APPROPRIATE BEHAVIOR

Parents get angry, too. How we handle our anger teaches our children how to handle *their* anger as well. So, how can we blow off some steam without losing our cool?

Go into a separate room where you can yell, kick, or pound a pillow.

Lie down on the floor in total surrender for few minutes.

Take a few deep breaths.

Laugh or cry.

Call a trusted friend who will listen to you with empathy and care.

Using Natural Consequences— Not Punishment

A toddler is in a constant state of discovery, curious and excited by new possibilities. What happens when we introduce punishment to their curious nature?

Children are wired for connection and attachment. When they are punished for their behavior, they are forced to direct their energy into mental and emotional survival. A system of punishment and reward tells a child that love is conditional. They must act a certain way for a parent to love and accept them. If they do not act this way, then this love can be removed, and they will be alone. This teaches them not to trust how they feel or what they want. They can trust only something separate from themselves.

Allowing children to experience the natural consequences of their actions teaches them to trust themselves to make decisions. Being the agent of their decisions helps them become comfortable learning from their "mistakes."

Benefits of Conscious Parenting

Conscious parenting won't just help you have a better relationship with your toddler; it will teach you to have a better relationship with yourself and those around you. This is a way of living that can enrich all aspects of your life. As you become more self-aware, you will learn to be less reactive to triggers and to self-regulate your emotions. Connection becomes the priority, rather than correcting behavior, with the impulse to reestablish connection whenever it breaks. As you start to live in the present moment, playfulness and gratitude abound.

SETTING APPROPRIATE GOALS _____

Setting appropriate parenting goals is not only helpful, it's a sign of self-love. The goal is not to be the best or most perfect parent. As conscious parents, it is important to acknowledge that today, this very moment, is all we have. We can choose to reconnect with the love for our children by reflecting that love. They are the mirror of this moment.

Wherever we are in our parenting journey, we are united by our desire to evolve and shift our mindset:

- ▸ We want to make progress in how we handle conflict and other difficult situations.
- ▸ We want to model self-discipline and self-awareness for our children instead of obedient compliance.
- ▸ We want to educate ourselves on our child's natural developmental stages so we don't overwhelm them with unreasonable expectations.
- ▸ We want to become mindful of external factors in our environment that we can or cannot control and act accordingly.
- ▸ We want to pay attention to our old story and detach from it one day at the time.

Self-Discipline, Not Compliance

Toddlers are dependent on us for survival, and we expect—and need—their compliance in order to help them survive. Yet this need for obedience is often the cause of parental stress and frustration. When we demand that a toddler learn to follow parental orders, or when we compel their obedience under threat, the results are temporary, while the negative effects of this authoritarian parenting harm the emotional connection.

When parents model self-discipline and awareness instead, toddlers will follow suit. We can show patience and restraint in a way that underscores those values. We can seek to understand our own motives and impulses before acting, teaching our young children to question themselves and others before acting out. And we can model gratitude and compassion, catching our triggers before they erupt and reminding ourselves that our emotional connection is the priority in each moment.

Developmental Considerations

During the toddler years and up through age seven, children cannot filter their conscious responses. They absorb everything around them as being true, real, and absolute. There *is* a monster under the bed. Imaginary friends are *very* real. And if a parent yells, a child takes that to mean they are unloved.

A child's whole environment impacts how they perceive themselves and the world around them. When their need for connection and safety is repeatedly unmet, they learn to adapt to an unsafe world.

How do we make the world safe for a toddler who perceives everything as real? Who doesn't understand why we're angry or what made us yell? We do this by investigating our own feelings and fears so that we are able to see that what really hurts us in a difficult parenting moment is not our child's behavior, but our own emotional triggers. When we set aside our reaction, we can choose to respond in a way that seeks to understand our little one's behavior and support our emotional connection.

MANTRA

These mantras are based on conscious parenting principles. Use them throughout your parenting journey to help strengthen your understanding and acceptance.

Whatever my child is reflecting back to me, I accept and embrace as part of myself. It is not good or bad. It simply is a part of me. If it doesn't serve me anymore, I can choose to let it go. I am a good parent and I will work for the purpose of growth and unconditional love.

CONSCIOUS PARENTING RECAP

1. Our children are generous teachers who guide us in the process of reclaiming our authenticity and personal power.

2. There are many approaches to conscious parenting. It is up to you to learn and adopt the principles that resonate with you.

3. We have a responsibility to ensure an emotionally safe environment for our kids.

4. We are responsible for healing our unresolved wounds so that we don't pass them on to our children.

5. Conscious parenting requires bravery. You are a brave parent.

REFLECTION QUESTIONS

1. What are my fears about my child?

2. What makes me lose my patience?

3. What am I ashamed of?

4. What do I fear people will say about me as a parent?

5. What qualities do I admire in other parents?

FIND CALM IN THE HEAT OF THE MOMENT

Finding calm when things are at their most stressful is one of the biggest challenges in parenting. When our emotions take over, we lose self-control. We stop thinking rationally and are no longer present. We forget how much we love our children, how vulnerable they are—and that they depend on us to feel safe and protected in the world.

Instead, we go into a state of mindlessness. We don't enter this state intentionally; it happens in the blink of an eye. When we lose our self-control, we lose our ability to self-regulate. And it can take hours, sometimes days, to get it back.

In this chapter, you'll learn how to find calm when emotions are spiraling out of control by learning how to catch these triggers and what to look for before they erupt.

SELF-REGULATING YOUR EMOTIONS

We have the best intentions with our kids, and we do our very best at any given moment. But every parent breaks the promise to not yell at their child. That's because stress hormones diminish our ability to think clearly and to connect to other people, even our children, making it difficult to regulate intense emotions when we feel triggered.

How can we self-regulate our emotions in the heat of the moment? Conscious parents will constantly ask the following questions:

- Who is this invisible master who takes control over me?
- Why am I not stronger?
- Where does my conscious mind go?
- Where does my unconditional love for my child go?

Asking these questions after a stressful, emotional encounter with our child is the difference between unconscious and conscious parenting.

Why is self-inquiry significant in conscious parenting? The parent who uses these questions to look within is aware that their explosive behavior is not truly who they are. The conscious parent understands that this reaction is a method of self-defense to an unconscious thought, hurt, or threat. Although how the child acted was a trigger, the child is not responsible.

Self-regulation in the heat of the moment is a skill that we can all learn to master. How we communicate with our children in moments of high tension teaches them the following:

- To trust us (or not)
- To feel safe with us (or not)

- To say how they feel and what's going on inside of them
- To come to us for safety (or to run away)
- To handle conflict the way we do
- To self-regulate the way we do

Children absorb their environment. They model how we behave—not what we tell them to do. This means that your toddler will model your behavior in the heat of the moment.

The Importance of Self-Care

Just as it's important to take good care of your child, it is vital that you practice that same level of care with yourself. This helps your mind and heart stay attuned to your toddler's needs and will lead to less reactivity on your part. Commit to one (or more) of the following self-care routines:

- Sleep six to eight hours per night.
- Eat nutritious food.
- Exercise regularly.
- Enjoy a hobby.
- Talk to another caring adult.
- Join a weekly parent support group.
- Meditate.
- Practice self-compassion.
- Practice gratitude.
- Spend quality time alone.
- Spend time with a partner or close friends.
- Spend time in nature.
- Keep a journal.
- Find a means of creative self-expression.

IDENTIFY YOUR BIGGEST TRIGGERS

Triggers are automatic responses to sudden changes that result in an uncontrolled emotional state. When something triggers you, you might say something like this:

"He pushed my buttons."

"I can't stand it when that happens."

"I totally lost my cool when . . ."

"I acted like a crazy person even though I knew better."

Most of us have experienced being triggered. By identifying your triggers, you can increase your levels of self-awareness and improve your relationships with your children, your partner, your relatives, other parents, teachers, and anyone else in your little one's life.

SELF-CHECK

In "Getting Started with Conscious Parenting," we learned the principles of conscious parenting and how they apply to our relationship not only with our toddler, but also with ourselves.

Conscious parenting is a commitment to bringing awareness to childhood hurts in order to integrate them through love and acceptance of the self. When you feel triggered and tempted to blame, review the principles in the "Getting Started" section.

We can also learn to stop our automatic response to these instances. The following pages explore some of the most common triggers parents might experience.

Crying and Whining

When an infant cries, our instinct is to nurture and soothe. Crying and fussing is how a newborn communicates that they need attention. Once they reach toddlerhood at 12 to 18 months, children start to learn a few words, begin to walk, and seek more independence.

With this independence, parents will start to unconsciously change their perception of crying or whining. We expect our child to say when they are hungry, tell us when they are tired, and ask when they want us to play. We tell them to stop crying when they are not really hurt or when we drop them off at daycare because we have to go to work.

We associate crying and whining with pain, so we assume that when a child cries, they are in some type of discomfort. If we cannot take away that pain, we must be "bad parents." Crying and whining trigger feelings of discomfort and emotional distress. We want the crying to stop so we can feel better about ourselves.

Why do we ask our children to stop crying? What is it about crying that makes us uncomfortable?

First, let's demystify the belief that crying equals pain. Instead, think of it as a healing process for all human beings. When a child cries, they are working to heal the pain that exists in their emotional body. What they need is unconditional acceptance and support from a loving adult in order to heal.

When our child cries and we cannot give them the support they need, we might have the following thoughts:

"I am failing as a parent."

"I can't help my child" or "I don't know how to help my child."

"What's all this fuss about? Nothing happened."

"Nobody was paying attention to me when I was crying, and I turned out okay."

"In my family, crying was a sign of weakness."

"Boys don't cry. He will grow up weak. He has to become a real man."

"Crying is for babies."

In response, we try to regain control by focusing on getting our children to stop crying and whining. We might ask nicely in a gentle tone of voice, or we might yell and scream. The lesson is the same:

Crying is not good. If you keep crying, you are not being good.

You need to shut down your natural instinct of healing because I feel distress when you cry.

I am not here for you when you cry.

You will learn to stop crying at my command if you want my love and attention.

Temper Tantrums

Temper tantrums are heavily associated with the toddler's "terrible twos." Parents are desperate to control their toddlers as they scream and cry, kick and throw things, or shout "NO" at the top of their lungs. The reality is that a tantrum is a desperate need for a parent's attention.

Why is a tantrum so terrible? When a child is engaged in this behavior, they are so frustrated that they are out of control. They cannot process information or think logically—and we feel powerless as parents.

WE WANT . . .	BUT WE CAN'T BECAUSE . . .
to fight with the child.	they are too young.
to convince them of reason.	they can't think logically.
to shut them down.	they are screaming louder than us.
to hold them.	they run away.
to warn them they can hurt themselves.	they don't seem to care.

Tantrums can trigger a feeling of powerlessness because others perceive tantrums as a parent's inability to control a child's unruly behavior. This lack of control can make us feel incapable or ashamed, which leads us to react in the following ways:

- Putting our child on time-out to "calm down"
- Yelling to stop the behavior

- Rewarding our little one only if they stop the behavior
- Punishing by taking away a toy or TV time
- Withholding love and affection

Punishing tantrums or rewarding the child if they shut down for us emotionally tells the toddler that their feelings are too big to handle. Then, the more they learn to deny their feelings of frustration, the more they will be rewarded.

Disobedience

Children need structure, rules, rituals, and predictability in order to feel safe in the world. When they defy or disobey these rules, it challenges a parent's role as the authority figure in the relationship. It's important to pay attention to what we think and how we feel when our toddler doesn't listen to us.

When a child disobeys, our unresolved feelings of incompetence or lack of worth can trigger an emotional reaction. When this happens, we are unable to be mindful. Instead, we want the following:

- To be listened to
- To feel we are in charge
- To believe that what we say is important
- To feel that we matter in the world
- To feel knowledgeable, competent, and prepared for what life throws at us

As a parent, we choose to punish or reward our child until they validate our self-worth.

Aggressive Behavior

Aggression is a natural manifestation of a feeling of anger that needs to be expressed.

Anger can scare a parent because it is explosive and unsafe in nature. Our instinct is to protect ourselves and our little one. Our fear is that, if we don't, the child will become more aggressive or turn into a bully.

Anger is a healthy emotion. It signals to the body that a physical, emotional, or mental boundary has been trespassed. When a toddler expresses anger or aggression, it means they feel out of balance. Something has happened that felt traumatic. It could be as simple as dropping an ice cream cone on the ground or losing a toy, or it can be more complex, such as a parent's divorce, the death of someone close, or moving to a new school.

Aggression and anger trigger our own fear response, which can result in an unloving reaction in the parent. We might have the following thoughts:

- ▸ "Anger is bad."
- ▸ "I was hurt by angry people."
- ▸ "Girls don't yell, scream, or fight. It's not feminine."
- ▸ "Kids must learn how to control their anger."
- ▸ "Angry people end up in bad relationships."
- ▸ "Angry people are bad people."

Punishing a toddler who is being aggressive tells them that something is wrong with them. Their anger is too frightening for us to create a safe space so they can feel their anger with you. Instead, they must shut down their anger in order to be loved and accepted.

Perceived Failure

Failure is fear-based thinking meant to control our behavior so that we can feel as though we "fit in." One of the ways failure controls our thinking is when we quantify and measure our success as parents through the achievements of our children. When we start putting pressure on them early in life to succeed, it only grows from there, until it becomes unbearable later on in life.

This behavior is actually our own fear of failure as a parent, which results in thoughts such as these:

- "This can't happen to my child."
- "I know they can do better than this."
- "If they fail now when life is easy, what will they do when things get hard?"
- "I can't let my child fail. It's my responsibility to see them succeed."
- "My toddler needs to keep up with the rest of the kids."
- "Getting into the best elementary school depends on this."
- "Getting good at something starts young."
- "Their future depends on this."
- "What would others think about me?"
- "I can't allow myself to fail as a parent."

When we pressure a "failing" child to succeed, this tells them that they are here to serve our needs. They are only as good as their performance (in school/sports/extra-curricular activities, etc.) or their results. Our worth as a parent is dependent on their performance; they must shine so that we can shine, too.

WHAT TO DO WHEN YOU FEEL TRIGGERED

Wouldn't it be wonderful if someone could give us a magic pill that solved what to do when we feel this way? Fortunately, there are steps we can take to prepare for the inevitable triggers of parenting.

HOW TO FIND CALM WHEN YOU LOSE YOUR COOL

Finding our calm in the moment is not easy. We must be proactive in prioritizing our self-care, while committing to bringing our awareness to the present moment in a high-tension situation.

When you lose your cool, take a few deep breaths. Hold the breaths in and then slowly release to a count of four. This helps calm the nervous system, which in turn helps us deescalate our response.

Practice Before Being Triggered

It's unrealistic to expect that we will have a clear mind and an open heart every time a conflict arises. As a conscious parent, it's important to prioritize and commit to our own self-care. Here are a few things you can do:

PRACTICE SIMPLE MEDITATION

Parents need time to be quiet and still, but many shy away when they hear the word "meditation." Don't worry, I'm not asking you to sit for hours on end. Start small with 5 to 10 minutes of alone time, then gradually increase to 15, 20, or 30 minutes. (Set a timer on your phone or use an app.) How long you sit is less important than the consistency and frequency of practice. During this time alone, your only goal is to be silent and stay in your own stillness. Your mind will flood with thousands of thoughts; let them come and go without resistance. Try to practice two or three times a week (or daily, if possible). Gradually you will begin to see the big picture in the heat of the moment and become less reactive.

PRACTICE GRATITUDE

My son and I share a gratitude mantra that we both say to each other every morning before we leave the house. It goes like this:

His version: *"Thank you for my wonderful life and my wonderful self and my wonderful mommy and daddy and my toys, friends, activities, and for all the love that I feel in my heart. I love you, Alexander. I am perfect just the way I am."*

My version: *"Thank you for my wonderful life and my wonderful self and my wonderful son, Alexander, and my wonderful family, friends, and work that support me in my growth. I love you, Mihaela. I am perfect just the way I am."*

Establishing a gratitude practice (either alone or with your child) is powerful because it offers the following reminders:

- We are a part of life as a whole.
- We are a part of something bigger than ourselves.
- We have the power to make choices every day.
- We are grateful to be the parent of our child.
- Our child is a gift to us.
- We model gratitude and humbleness for our children.
- We model self-love for our children.

A gratitude practice helps you start the day feeling grateful. Consider keeping a gratitude journal and writing this practice in it every morning or in the evening before going to bed.

PRACTICE LISTENING

Spend 30 minutes each week with a friend or another parent who can offer a safe and nonjudgmental space where you can both express your anger, sadness, frustration, and disappointment in yourselves, your children, or even your partners. Commit to listening without offering advice. This regular practice clears our minds and opens our hearts for connection.

Tips and Techniques for When You Feel Triggered

All tips and techniques will both work and fail, depending on the situation, your level of reactivity, and the level of your child's emotional distress. These are meant as a guide to help get you started in your own conscious parenting, as well as continue to change and grow along with your child. For each technique, it is helpful to bring your awareness back into the present moment by breathing deeply three or four times to re-center your body and mind.

WHEN YOU FEEL LIKE SCREAMING OR CRYING

Take a five-minute time-out. Make sure your child is safe (either alone or with another adult), then say, "I love you, but I need a few minutes alone." Leave the room and, once alone, scream into a pillow or hit and kick the couch or a bed. If you feel like crying, allow yourself to do so. This is your body releasing the hurt that clutters your thinking.

WHEN YOU START TO BARGAIN

Remember that you are the adult in the relationship; your job is to keep your child safe by setting firm but loving limits. Lower yourself so that you are at eye level with your child, which sends a nonverbal signal that you are on their side (and not against them). In a gentle tone of voice, set a firm limit with love. For example: "I can't let you have a second ice cream and watch another episode of TV. But I'll stay with you until you feel better."

WHEN YOU ASSUME NEGATIVE INTENT

Always remember that toddlers are incapable of negative intent. (The prefrontal cortex of their brain is not fully developed to do so.) When they oppose us, they are simply trying to learn and discover the world around them. Instead of assuming negative intent, be curious. Ask yourself, "What is my child looking for/ thinking/wanting to discover?" "How can I help?" "How can I best serve this growing mind in this moment?"

WHEN YOU WANT TO BLAME

Blame leads to guilt and shame. A child who feels guilty and ashamed will lose their confidence and sense of personal power. Instead, turn the mirror inward and ask yourself, "How could I have helped my child before this happened?" "Was I present with my child before this happened?" "What was my child's need when they did/said . . . ?" "Who was there for them if I wasn't?"

WHEN YOU FEEL GUILTY OR ASHAMED

Don't run away from these feelings. They are a light in the darkness of parenting. Ask yourself, either in the moment or later, "When did I feel guilty or ashamed as a child?" "Who made me feel this way?" "Who was there for me when I felt guilty or ashamed?" "Can I reconnect with myself as this child and show that I love them?"

Keep a photo of yourself as a child somewhere you will see it every day. Look at this photo and send unconditional love and acceptance to your younger self.

WHEN YOU WANT TO LECTURE

Remember that connection must come before correction. This principle will pay off in the long run because it helps you build a lifelong relationship with your child. When you want to lecture, leave the room for a few minutes, ask for a hug, or simply lie down on the floor and say nothing. Your child might even join you. Then address the "lesson" later when you are calm and fully centered.

MANTRA

Whatever I feel in the heat of the moment is a valid feeling. I will embrace my emotions. My child is the mirror I need to heal. I am in my power when I choose to connect instead of react.

STEP 1 RECAP

1. It is our subconscious mind, which is formed in the first seven years of life, that reacts in the heat of the moment. Our childhood environment determined our present "personalities."

2. The way we react in the heat of the moment during our child's toddler years determines the relationship we will have with them in their teenage years and beyond.

3. Triggers are automatic, and sudden changes in our emotional state lead to uncontrollable behaviors.

4. When we become conscious of our triggers, we can transform ourselves from the inside out.

5. There is no "magic pill" to cure our reactivity in the heat of the moment. It takes commitment, daily practice, and humility to transition from unconsciousness to consciousness. This work will pay off in unimaginable ways for both you and your child.

REFLECTION QUESTIONS

1. What are my biggest triggers? (Choose two.)

2. When am I most prone to being triggered?

3. What are the recurring thoughts, memories, or feelings that surface when I feel triggered?

4. Do I take care of myself in a committed way?

5. Do I have any rituals that fill me with love and connection?

UNDERSTAND YOUR TODDLER'S BEHAVIOR

Parenting is a long journey, and every day is an opportunity for learning and self-discovery. Understanding a toddler's behavior can help us become more aware of our own emotional triggers and reactions.

A child is a mirror that reflects back the unresolved wounds and fear-based patterns hidden within ourself, bringing those negative feelings to the surface.

In this chapter, you'll learn how to help your toddler (and yourself) by understanding, managing, and healing your own triggers. Once you become aware of these feelings, you can start to respond rather than react. As a result, when your toddler is in the heat of a tantrum or meltdown, you can tune in to their perspective and empathize with their needs, emotions, and curiosity.

YOUR TODDLER AND YOU

Toddlerhood is a beautiful and complex stage in a child's physical, cognitive, emotional, social and interpersonal development. The American Academy of Pediatrics delineates the toddler phase from one to three years of age, with distinct developmental milestones at 18 months, 24 months, and 36 months regarding gross and fine motor skills, language skills, and intellectual abilities. For example, a two-year-old is able to formulate a two- to three-word sentence ("I am beautiful." "Give me that!"), while a three-year-old can plan and organize a full pretend game (playing doctor, mom, dad, or teacher) as a way to tell a story. Equally significant is that by the age of three, a toddler's physical abilities will allow for independent movement, exploration, and ever-increasing curiosity about the world around them.

Becoming aware of these subtle developmental characteristics allows us to be fully present so that we can provide the safe emotional space a toddler needs in difficult moments. Once we understand the inner world of our child, we can show up from a place of love and empowerment. So, what do we know about our toddler's changes?

- A toddler has become aware that they are a separate self (individual) from the primary caregiver. This means that the strive for **autonomy** and **independence** is the main driver for all behavior.
- A toddler's language skills are advancing rapidly; however, toddlers are incapable of verbalizing their needs and emotions. They will use **behavior** to communicate, primarily through temper tantrums, aggression, lack of cooperation, and a resistance to rules and structure.
- A toddler is a **magical thinker**—they use symbols and imagination. They have not yet learned to distinguish between reality and fantasy.
- A toddler is beginning to actively master **impulse control** (for example, toilet training).
- A toddler's foundation of **self-esteem** and **personal will** is being built and depends entirely on the response from their caregiver.
- The toddler's impulse is to **explore**—they want to feel independent.
- A toddler needs **secure attachment** and **connection** with their caregiver.

SELF-CHECK

In **step 1**, we learned how triggers work and why it is difficult to stay present in the heat of the moment. Conscious parenting is a journey within that teaches self-awareness and humility. It is okay to stumble, fall, and make mistakes, as long as we remain committed to learning about ourselves in the process.

Whenever you find yourself in an emotionally charged situation with your toddler and unable to think clearly in the moment, refer back to **step 1**. Remember:

▸ Your child's safety comes first.

▸ Once your child is safe, take time to center yourself and come back to the present.

▸ Gain perspective on the situation so that you can rebuild connection with yourself and your child.

OVERVIEW OF COMMON MISBEHAVIORS

Even though toddlers are small, their feelings are big! Their brains are learning at an incredibly fast rate, working hard to process new information each second. All this information can often feel in conflict with their innate drive for autonomy and independence. Being unable to verbally express their emotions and frustrations can lead to what is commonly labeled as "misbehavior."

Common toddler "misbehaviors" include temper tantrums, indignation, aggressiveness (hitting, biting, pushing), crying, refusing to collaborate with others or follow routines and rituals, and rigid behaviors over prolonged periods (for example, your child will eat only one food).

In conscious parenting, we prefer the term "disconnected behavior" because the toddler isn't doing anything wrong. They are trying to communicate the only way they can that "something doesn't feel right" and "I need help." Understanding this allows us to meet our toddler with full acceptance and to reestablish connection. We can be fully present without judging their emotional state, reassuring them that we are there for them no matter what. This approach is the foundation of a relationship based on connection and unconditional love.

> Toddlers are trying to communicate the only way they can that "something doesn't feel right" and "I need help."

Tantrums

This seemingly irrational behavior is the result of an exasperated toddler who is unable to accept their limitations, such as being unable to reach a high shelf, carry a heavy toy, or read a book without assistance. But limitations can also be imposed on toddlers by others. A parent or other caregiver often controls their food choices and bedtime. A child may be forced to share a parent's love and attention with a sibling.

During a temper tantrum, a toddler may scream, kick, yell, pound their fists, cry inconsolably—all while refusing a parent's help, leaving Mom or Dad feeling powerless and without options. A child uses this tantrum-like behavior to communicate a feeling of helplessness or a state of panic, and needs to be helped, understood, and validated. (For tips on dealing with tantrums, see the "Common Behaviors and Conflicts" chapter.)

Anger

Anger is one emotion that scares parents due to its explosive, volcanic, and seemingly destructive nature. Yet anger is healthy. It can signal a perceived threat to a toddler's personal safety, be it physical, emotional, or mental. It can look like a parent leaving for work, a snack that falls on the floor, or the family pet hiding under the bed. When this triggers an angry reaction, this indicates a toddler's need for their internal compass to point back to a feeling of safety and control.

Parents who were not allowed to express anger as children may not have the skills to embrace anger in others as a healthy emotion. Teaching toddlers how to safely express anger gives them a foundation for feeling empowered so they can learn to fearlessly protect themselves as they grow older. (For tips on dealing with anger and aggression, see the "Common Behaviors and Conflicts" chapter.)

Negative Oppositional Behaviors

Toddlers need to discover the world around them. The way they do this is to oppose the parent. Oppositional behaviors are neither negative nor positive. They are simply a stage in a toddler's development where they begin to learn how to make personal choices and feel in control.

Parents must allow their young children to disagree with them. It is possible to allow a toddler to be oppositional while also holding a firm but gentle limit on their behavior, but it takes practice, a calm mind, and empathic communication. (For tips on dealing with oppositional behaviors, see the "Common Behaviors and Conflicts" chapter.)

STEP 2

Impulsive Behaviors

Impulsiveness is an immediate, unfiltered, and uncontrolled reaction to something that a toddler wants right now. It shows up in behaviors such as grabbing, pushing, breaking, or tearing something apart in frustration.

Toddlers are unable to wait for something or to think long-term. They live in the present moment, and their impulsive reactions are a way for them to communicate a need for attention and the validation of their desire. (For tips on dealing with a lack of impulse control, see the "Common Behaviors and Conflicts" chapter.)

Possessiveness

"MINE!" Sound familiar? If so, consider what the declaration really means. By claiming possession of toys, an object, or personal space, a toddler is securing a place in their world. What triggers this possessive behavior is a toddler's realization that they are separate from others, which leads to a profound shift in how a toddler perceives the world.

This is a powerful step in their development. As their separateness is validated by those around them, children begin to feel more connected to their identity and inner voice. This gives them the confidence to trust who they are and stand up for themselves. (For tips on dealing with a refusal to share, see the "Common Behaviors and Conflicts" chapter.)

Aggressive Behaviors

Aggressive behavior is one way that a toddler manifests their anger. It can result in hitting, pushing, kicking, pulling hair, biting, spitting, and tearing or destroying toys or other objects.

These are all signs of a child who is scared. They are crippled by a fear that they do not have the language to communicate but that is very present in the body. By using aggressive behavior, a toddler is attempting to escape the prison of their fear, whether real or imagined.

Some of the things that can cause this feeling are a major life event such as a divorce or the loss of a loved one, or it could be something relatively simple like the sudden bark of a dog or the loss of a toy. The source of the fear is not important. It's the need behind it that parents must pay attention to—the need to feel safe and unconditionally loved. (For tips on dealing with aggression, see the "Common Behaviors and Conflicts" chapter.)

EXECUTIVE FUNCTIONING SKILLS

It's possible to become very attached to our goals for "good parenting." We want to set our children up for success and happiness, and we can do that only by teaching them how to self-regulate and make good decisions. While this may sound like a good plan, it is not aligned with conscious parenting.

Executive functioning skills are highly desirable in our society. They reflect a well-rounded individual who can manage their emotions and make good judgments that are win-win for everybody. But managing our emotions in the heat of the moment is difficult, even for parents who practice mindfulness or meditation.

The only way to teach our children executive functioning skills is to model them ourselves.

Executive Functioning

Executive functioning is the brain's ability to plan and execute a cognitive task. Our brains integrate working memory, inhibitory control (i.e., self-control), and mental flexibility in order to plan, problem solve, and make decisions.

We expect these functions from our children, but as adults we often fail to demonstrate them ourselves. We yell, we scold, and we want things our way and resist anything different.

Conscious parenting invites you to reflect on your own executive functioning skills. By the time we become parents, we may have developed a strong working memory, but what about our inhibitory control and mental flexibility? What happens when we feel triggered?

Unless we become aware of this, we will be unable to self-regulate in the moment. It's important to identify our triggers so that we are aware of when we are most vulnerable to feeling triggered. Ask yourself the following:

- Is there a certain moment of the day when I feel most triggered?
- Is there a certain word or behavior from my child that pushes my buttons?

- Is it when I am sleep- or food-deprived that I lack patience or empathy for myself or my child?
- Is it when my needs for support and connection are not being met that I react, only to regret it later?
- Is it when I feel alone and/or overwhelmed as a parent that I can't control my reactions?

Writing down these questions can be a powerful exercise. Sometimes we need this practice in order to have the time and space to feel what we need, remember our own childhood, and slow our thinking in order to discover the source of our triggers.

Noticing and becoming aware of what triggers us improves our executive functioning skills. When we are in control of our mind and reactions, we can demonstrate the mental flexibility required to plan, problem solve, and make good decisions. We are no longer the prisoners of our reactive thoughts.

It is in the toddler years that a parent can model these executive functioning skills in order to plant the seeds of what it will take for their child to live a secure and happy life. A toddler's young mind will absorb what we model for them.

The conscious modeling of behavior *is* conscious parenting. When we model executive functioning skills for our toddlers, we do the following:

- Demonstrate self-control of our behavior
- Regulate our explosive emotions in the moment
- Become aware of our triggers in the moment
- Identify past emotional hurts and connect them with our parenting triggers
- Show flexibility of mind (explore options, vary behaviors, demands, and expectations)
- Practice self-care to maintain our own love and connection

SETTING THE GROUNDWORK

Setting the groundwork for children to acquire well-developed executive functioning skills starts with what we can model for them each day.

The ages of 18 to 36 months are important stepping-stones in the development of a child's working memory, self-regulation, and mental flexibility. Their young brains create neural pathways based on repetitive behavior and perceptions. As a child is repeatedly exposed to skills that support secure attachment and connection, they will learn to model that behavior, and their executive functioning skills will thrive.

Secure Attachment

A child whose needs are consistently and predictably met feels safe and secure. They learn to direct their energy toward mastering memory, self-regulating, and learning how to be mentally flexible. If a child's needs are not met or are neglected, they will feel unsafe and insecure. Their energy will be focused on survival in the face of fear, loneliness, and unpredictability, and their cognitive development may become disorganized.

SELF-CHECK

Secure attachment and emotional connection are both important to conscious parenting. To learn how to establish emotional connection, review **steps 3** and **4**. To understand your toddler's behavior, reread **step 2**.

The Role of Emotional Regulation

Toddlers depend on their parents and primary caregivers to wire their brains for emotional connection and secure attachment. The way a parent can model emotional regulation is by listening to a child when their distressed emotions arise, sending the message that we are there for them, no matter what.

Using Language

As your toddler learns to develop speech, you can begin to teach them some simple language that they can use in order to communicate their emotions and feelings. Using short, simple words in combination with games, role-playing, and storytelling is a fun and engaging way to help a toddler understand what is happening and why, and to give them space to respond.

When initiating play, follow your child's lead. Let them use role-play to tell you what scared, upset, and frustrated them. You can also use stuffed animals or hand puppets to help them tell a story or ask easy questions.

Read aloud to your child and choose storybooks that explore their inner life, thoughts, and feelings. As you read, model awareness and emotional regulation by asking questions like these:

- ▸ What do you think the character in the story is feeling? What do you feel right now?
- ▸ What do you think this character is thinking? What are you thinking right now?
- ▸ What do you think this character needs? Is there anything you need right now?
- ▸ What do you think this character wants? Is there anything you want right now?

Though your child may lack the speech development or language skills to respond to these questions, it's the *asking* that's important. By teaching them to ask how they think and feel, and to reflect on their wants and needs, we can teach them to become aware of their emotions in the moment.

MANTRA

I am the perfect parent for my child and my child is the perfect child for me. I embrace all of my emotions and all of my child's emotions. I cherish and honor the present moment with my child.

STEP 2 RECAP

1. A toddler is totally dependent on parents and caretakers to develop a sense of safety and security in the world.

2. A toddler's development is impacted by how parents respond to their behavior.

3. A toddler uses emotional outbursts ("misbehaviors") to communicate that something doesn't feel good inside.

4. The way a parent self-regulates helps model emotional regulation in their child.

5. Toddlers need secure attachment in order to develop executive functioning skills.

REFLECTION QUESTIONS

1. Do I have a good understanding of how my toddler thinks and communicates emotions?

2. Do I have reasonable or unreasonable expectations for my toddler?

3. Do I model self-regulation well?

4. Do I model mental flexibility well?

5. What aspects of my self-regulation do I need to change?

6. What aspects of my mental flexibility do I need to change?

ESTABLISH A FEELING OF SAFETY

The ultimate goal of conscious parenting is to raise children who feel worthy of love simply for being themselves. A child who grows up feeling safe— physically, emotionally, and mentally—develops a strong sense of self that feels worthy of unconditional love and acceptance in the world. This child will become an adult who sees their unlimited potential; who is kind and generous, resilient and innovative in the face of adversity.

In this chapter, we'll examine some toddler behaviors that often result from overstimulation or a perceived threat. Each behavior includes easy-to-remember tools for establishing a feeling of safety that can be used in the moment.

HOW TO HELP
YOUR CHILD FEEL SAFE

Feeling safe is as vital to a young child as food and water. There are many facets that lead to this:

PHYSICAL. Children feel safe when nothing threatens their body and physical well-being. The basic needs for food, shelter, and physical protection are met on a consistent basis, and in a predictable way, by the adults around them. This child learns to trust that, if they are ever in harm's way, someone will be there to protect them.

EMOTIONAL. Children feel safe when they are fully accepted for who they are, especially in difficult moments of emotional meltdowns. A child's emotional safety is the result of their daily interactions with a parent or adult. Children learn to trust their environment when the adults in their life listen and offer empathy.

MENTAL. Children feel safe when they learn to embrace and make sense of the world inside their mind. When thoughts and feelings are accepted and understood by loving parents and caretakers, it gives appropriate meaning to events, people, and relationships. This child learns to integrate the experiences of their life into a story that makes sense. If they start to cry when one parent leaves for work, the other parent (or babysitter) can accept this feeling and say, "I can see that you are sad someone left for work, even though they go to work every day. I can hold you until you feel better."

You love your child. However, love is not enough to be a conscious parent. Love without self-awareness and presence of mind can lead to behaviors that may not support your child.

It's important to identify our triggers as parents, become aware of what our "hot buttons" are, and integrate our triggers by making sense of the painful stories from our past. When you are overtaken by anger, rage, or resentment, you cannot help your child (and might even jeopardize your child's emotional safety).

You can prevent this from happening. Revisit the strategies to "Find Calm in the Heat of the Moment" in **step 1.**

RESPONDING TO WITHDRAWAL

Toddlers are like blooming flowers. Their bodies are growing, their brains are developing at a rapid speed, and as they learn how the world around them works, they begin to use language to communicate. Their cognitive abilities are still limited, however, and this can feel frustrating both for themselves and for their parents.

Toddlers communicate through behavior.

Toddlers communicate through behavior. A toddler who is overwhelmed by anger, frustration, fear, or disappointment has no cognitive capacity to say "I feel terrified. I feel alone. I feel confused. I feel frustrated. I feel sad." Instead, they will use behaviors like withdrawal or aggression.

Lack of Eye Contact

A toddler relies on eye contact and nonverbal cues to ensure that they are loved and cared for. When a toddler avoids eye contact, it means that they feel disconnected and alone. This is a very frightening feeling for a young child. They want to feel better but don't know how. They need help.

HOW TO ESTABLISH A FEELING OF SAFETY

To help your child feel safe and secure, you can do the following:

- ▸ Stay close to your child. Allow your child to follow their body's need to move, cry, lie down, or play undisturbed with a toy.
- ▸ Offer warm attention through eye contact or gentle touch.
- ▸ Say, "I am here. I love you. Whenever you are ready, I am here to hold you in my arms."
- ▸ Lower yourself to be on the same level with your child, such as on the floor.
- ▸ Stay with your child until they have calmed down.

These tools will eventually help your child's emotional brain pick up on your warm and loving presence and will lead them to reconnect with you.

SIGNS OF OTHER FACTORS AT PLAY

While all the mentioned behaviors are typical for toddlers, some parents might be concerned there is something more going on. According to the organization Autism Speaks, here are some of the early signs of autism in toddlers:

- ▸ Little or no words or two-word phrases (by 24 months)

- ▸ Little or no back-and-forth gestures (pointing, reaching, waving, etc.)

- ▸ Little or no response to their own name

- ▸ Avoidance of eye contact

- ▸ Constant desire to be alone

- ▸ Resistance to minor changes in routine or settings

- ▸ Repetition of certain behaviors or words/phrases

- ▸ Unusual and intense reactions to sounds, smells, tastes, textures, lights, or colors

Of course, all children develop at their own pace. If you have any worries or questions about your child's progress, please consult your pediatrician immediately.

Resistance to Touch

Touch is a basic need for children. When a toddler refuses to be touched or held, it means that they feel isolated and disconnected, and are trying to protect themselves from a perceived threat.

It's difficult not to take it personally when your child rejects your affection. You might interpret this as rejection, but remember that it's your own wounds of rejection that you're feeling. Though young children need touch in order to feel connected to us, we cannot force it on them.

HOW TO ESTABLISH A FEELING OF SAFETY

To help your child feel safe and secure, you can do the following:

- Lower yourself to eye level with your child.
- Use eye contact, smile, and use open body language (open arms, smiling, and showing a desire to connect).
- Join your child in their activity while respecting their need for physical boundaries.
- Speak softly. Say, "I love you no matter what. I love playing with you. Whenever you feel ready, I will be right here to hold you. Nobody will force you to do what you don't want to do with your body."
- Softly hug a stuffed animal and invite your child to join you. If your child refuses, accept that and keep offering eye contact.
- Initiate an easy game. Say, "I really need a hug from somebody" in a needy but playful tone. A game can "unfreeze" your toddler's feeling of isolation.

It's important to be open to rejection. When a toddler avoids the invitation to play or hug, it means they need more time to feel safe. Being playful in difficult moments may sound counterintuitive, but play is the innate language of children.

Running Away or Hiding

When you are rushing to work, need to take care of another child, or are in the middle of the grocery store with a full cart, dealing with a toddler who is running away or trying to hide can be difficult. Ensuring their physical safety is the first priority, but a toddler who is running away or hiding also needs to release tension and stress.

HOW TO ESTABLISH A FEELING OF SAFETY

To help your child feel safe and secure, you can do the following:

- Be gentle but firm. Tell them, "I can't let you run in the street because it's dangerous." Hold your child so that they don't put themselves in harm's way again.
- If your child begins to cry or protest, be patient but keep them close to you.
- Find a safe space where your child can run and hide, free from danger.
- Join your child in play and turn their response into a game of hide-and-seek. Pretend that you can't find them and then let them emerge victorious.

Play is a great way to release tension and stress. Follow your child's laughter, smile, and maintain eye contact from a safe distance. Repeat the game a few times and remain open to new twists and turns.

Crying

Crying is a healing process that releases sadness, tension, and grief. When a toddler is crying, your best and necessary response is to listen.

HOW TO ESTABLISH A FEELING OF SAFETY
To help your child feel safe and secure, you can do the following:

- Remember, crying may take a while before it stops. Don't rush it.
- Stay close. Remain available to hold your child or softly touch them.
- Speak less. What you say should be unrelated to the reason for crying, such as: "You are safe now. I am here with you. I know this feels hard right now. I love you."
- Maintain eye contact.
- Let your child lead their healing process; avoid imposing any agenda.

Whining

When a toddler is whining, it means they feel lost, helpless, and confused. The child is in a state of helplessness and is asking for assistance. Your best response is to be curious, attentive, and patient. Notice, observe, and stay open, even when they ask for irrational or ridiculous things in their search for help.

STEP 3

HOW TO ESTABLISH A FEELING OF SAFETY

To help your child feel safe and secure, you can do the following:

- ▸ Realize that your child is genuinely asking for help and not trying to manipulate you.
- ▸ Be firm but gentle. Say, "I am sorry . . . I can't let you have another cookie today. I'll stay here with you until you feel better."
- ▸ Remain calm and offer warm attention, even as your child screams, cries, or protests.
- ▸ Allow your child to follow their body's way of letting go of heavy feelings, even if that means crying.

Limits allow a toddler to access and then release feelings of frustration and helplessness, allowing you to reestablish the emotional safety your toddler is looking for.

HANDLING PHYSICAL AGGRESSION

Anger is a big and scary feeling in toddlers and children of all ages. An angry child is a scared child who needs help to feel emotionally safe and connected. Physical aggression such as screaming, stomping, spitting, biting, scratching, hitting, kicking, and pushing are a toddler's way of communicating one thing: "I feel scared. I feel alone and isolated. I can't feel anybody's love for me. I am desperate for attention, love, and connection. Please help me!"

AN ANGRY CHILD IS . . .

- A hurt child

- A scared child

- A frightened child

- A child who feels helpless and powerless

- A child who can't reason logically

- A child who can't feel the love of parents, teachers, siblings, or other caretakers

- A child who can't verbalize the fear that they feel in their body

- A child who may or may not have conscious memories of where their fear is coming from

- A child who is releasing grief

- A child who wants to get rid of the fear in their body

- A child who will target their anger toward an adult with whom they feel safe

- A child who needs a firm but loving limit in order not to hurt themselves or others

- A child who needs your help

Screaming

When your toddler is screaming at the top of their lungs, you may feel triggered to scream back. You may feel embarrassed or ashamed as your child yells in public or even privately at home during dinner. Where does this feeling of shame come from?

When your child is screaming, self-awareness is key—an awareness of your fears and limitations about what others will think of you. These are issues you can work on with a therapist, a life coach, or by sitting in meditation and journaling.

Conscious parenting is a relationship based on safety, trust, honesty, presence of mind, and connection. Your job is not to control your child, but to be present with them.

HOW TO ESTABLISH A FEELING OF SAFETY
To help your child feel safe and secure, you can do the following:

- Remain calm. Assess the situation at hand. If your child is safe and unharmed, move your attention to their emotional needs.
- Allow your child to use their body to release strong feelings; screaming is a form of release.
- If your child's screaming violates another's sense of safety, move your child to a private place like another area of the playground, your car, or a bathroom. Do this gently and with love; it should not feel like a punishment.
- Say, "I am here with you now. Whatever scared you, it's gone now. You are not alone anymore. You are safe now. I love you."
- Give your child a pillow or a soft toy to scream into.

- Let your child cry. Stay close and hug them until the crying is over. You can say, "I am right here with you. You are safe now. I love you so much."

Hitting and Hurting

As with all aggressive behavior, hitting, biting, scratching, kicking, and pushing others are cries for help. They indicate that feelings of disconnection, fear, or hurt are taking over your toddler's playful and good-hearted nature.

When your toddler attempts to lash out physically, it may be tempting to put them in time-out, take away a privilege, or threaten them with a world-ending measure that will make their life miserable. These punishments don't work and can even damage your relationship with your child.

HOW TO ESTABLISH A FEELING OF SAFETY

To help your child feel safe and secure, you can do the following:

- Remain calm. Remind yourself that your child needs your help.
- Come close to your toddler and hold their hands or take them into your arms to keep everyone safe.
- Set a limit, letting your child know that hitting is unacceptable. This helps your child access the feelings behind their aggression. They may protest or cry.
- Stay close and listen; don't rush or lecture. Say, "I am right here with you. I am sorry this feels so hard for you right now. You are safe. I love you."

Stomping

Stomping is an expression of frustration or anger. Toddlers do this to release strong feelings that are bottled up inside their body.

If your toddler is in a safe place and the stomping won't disturb anyone, allow them to release their anger or frustration. If you are in a public place, move your child somewhere more private like another room, your car, or a bathroom. Do this gently and with love; it should not feel like a punishment. Then allow them to release their anger and frustration.

PREVENTING AGGRESSIVE BEHAVIORS

The following preventive practices can contribute to building a love- and trust-based relationship with your child:

- ▸ Make a habit of spending one-on-one time with your child every day.
- ▸ Introduce roughhousing or play before bedtime as part of a nighttime routine.
- ▸ Listen to and allow your child to finish their emotional off-loads (crying, yelling, tantrums) instead of immediately trying to calm them down or stop the behavior.
- ▸ Help your child manage their anger by letting them kick or yell into a pillow.

Make Time for Your Toddler

Spend one-on-one time with your child every day, even if only for 5 or 10 minutes. Engage your child in coming up with a fun name for your time together.

Use this time to play games or do any activity your child wants to do. Let them feel empowered and in control.

Make Time for Play

With so much to do, parents can find it a challenge to be naturally playful, but this is a learnable skill (really!). Don't be afraid to make fun of yourself to show your child that life isn't always so serious. Be sure to use humor and laughter whenever possible. Here are some ideas on how to inject fun into your day:

- Pretend that you are incapable of doing a task and desperately need your child's help.
- Write or draw little love notes to a child who is upset.
- Dress up in funny outfits or mismatched clothes.
- Say, "I don't know—let's find out together." Then you and your child can track down the answer together.
- Spend some time roughhousing together. (In conscious parenting, "roughhousing" simply means physical play that helps stimulate a child's brain and body.)

MANTRA

I am a good parent and I have a good child.
My child's unpleasant behavior is a cry for help.
I commit to taking care of myself every day so that
I can take care of my child.

STEP 3 RECAP

1. Withdrawal and aggression communicate that your child has unmet needs.

2. Your child needs your love and attention, especially in aggressive moments.

3. An aggressive child feels deeply scared, frightened, and isolated.

4. Only a loving parent or caretaker can help a child heal the fear that underpins aggression.

5. Playfulness is a learnable skill for any parent.

REFLECTION QUESTIONS

1. How did my parents treat me when I was angry/aggressive?

2. Who does my child remind me of when they try to hit or kick me?

3. What is the one aggressive behavior that is most difficult for me to stay calm in the face of?

4. How hard is it for me to listen to my child cry? Why?

5. How hard is it to see my child raging with anger? Why?

CONNECT EMOTIONALLY

Human beings are wired for connection. It is a primordial need as important as shelter, food, and water. This is why the parent-child connection is at the heart of conscious parenting. It is fundamental to a child's harmonious development and well-being.

When a child feels threatened, either physically or emotionally, their behavior can become chaotic, irrational, or aggressive. (We sometimes call this "bad behavior," but no child is "bad.") While caught in the middle of a tantrum, crying, or engaged in aggressive behavior, they simply cannot connect emotionally.

In this chapter, you'll learn how your toddler processes these feelings and why they react with emotional disconnection or aggressive behavior. A child caught in an emotionally intense episode or this kind of behavior needs help reconnecting with a caring adult. Understanding this can help parents have empathy and patience with toddlers in moments of irrational behavior.

EMOTIONAL CONNECTIONS AND THE BRAIN

To understand your child's behavioral responses, let's examine three systems of the human brain: the reptilian brain, the limbic system, and the prefrontal cortex. When these three systems are in harmony, a child is in an integrated state of mind: happy, collaborative, flexible, and open to learn. If a child feels threatened or unsafe, their brain will trigger a flight-or-fight response, and all executive functions stop. It doesn't matter if the triggering event happened in the past or present, if it was conscious or unconscious, the reaction is the same: "I am in danger. I am alone."

THE REPTILIAN BRAIN. This is the oldest part of the brain and it includes the brain stem and the cerebellum. Its main function is to keep us alive in the face of immediate danger. This part of our brain is about self-preservation.

THE LIMBIC SYSTEM. The limbic system includes the hippocampus and the amygdala. It is a part of the brain that supports our emotional life, such as our connection with others and identifying primary attachment figures (i.e., parents). It governs emotions, memories, and our experiences of fear. It helps us interpret nonverbal information, such as facial expressions or tone of voice, to decide whether to feel emotionally safe.

Infants and toddlers constantly look at a parent or caregiver's face to assure their emotional safety. This attunement (or "limbic resonance") can be a smile or a soft word that reassures them that everything is fine.

THE PREFRONTAL CORTEX. The prefrontal cortex includes the frontal lobe and is the youngest, and largest, part of our brain. It houses executive functions, such as cognitive behavior, abstract thinking, reason and logic, and impulse control (self-regulation).

SELF-CHECK

A toddler needs help to feel an emotional bond with you. But when you feel triggered, you cannot help your child in that moment. Walk away or breathe deeply four to eight times, count to 10, or lie down to calm your nervous system. Then return to **steps 1, 2,** and **3** to find a tool that works for you in this moment.

Children need to feel both physically and emotionally safe. A child feels emotionally safe when they are nurtured, validated, seen, and heard by the adults in their life.

RESPONDING TO ATTENTION-SEEKING BEHAVIORS

"Attention-seeking" behaviors include clinging, neediness, spitting, calling someone a name (maybe even you), and talking or yelling back instead of responding. In conscious parenting, we consider these "attention-needing" behaviors. It is the need behind the behavior that we must identify and meet.

> A toddler is trying to communicate an unmet need the only way they know how. It is the need behind the behavior that we must identify and meet.

All toddler behavior is a form of communication, even behavior we might label "negative." When your toddler is constantly clinging to you or whining for "no reason," they are trying to communicate an unmet need the only way they know how. In difficult moments, it is hard for a parent to remember to connect with their toddler before reacting to their behavior. Emotional connection is not possible when we are caught in the sticky web of unconscious triggers.

Clinging and Neediness

A toddler's natural desire is to be independent from the parent, to explore on their own and to learn to exist separate from you. But with this independence comes fear—of the unknown or the new.

Neediness comes from unresolved fear. When your child clings to you, it's because they need more of you and your attention. The emotional connection needs refilling.

To help your toddler, you can do the following:

- Look for patterns of clinginess. Does it primarily happen in the mornings before drop-off at daycare or with a babysitter? In the evening before bedtime? When another child has your attention? When another parent leaves for work?
- Now that you understand the pattern, you can learn to anticipate their clinginess. Build in time to connect, listen, hug, and reassure before these moments occur.
- Set aside some daily one-on-one time. Use it to do whatever your child wants.
- Spend 5 to 10 minutes in physical play, such as pillow fights, playing with soft toys, wrestling, or tickling. Laugher releases fear and restores self-confidence.

Spitting

The toddler years are a time of experimentation and exploration. It's a time when they copy what they see around them. If your toddler is spitting, it's possible that they picked this up from another child, or even an adult.

Spitting can be very hard for parents to handle. It's often associated with rudeness, disgust, repulsion, and aggression. If your toddler is engaging in this behavior, take time to pause and self-reflect. Ask yourself these questions:

1. What is the meaning that I give to this action?

2. How do I feel when my child spits on me?

3. How do I feel when my child spits on others?

4. What is my child reminding me of when they do this?

5. What is my earliest memory around spitting and what is that memory about?

If spitting has become a habitual attention-seeking behavior, a parent can look for patterns in the behavior. First consider, when does this happen? Is it triggered by an event or is it in response to imposed control or restriction? Once you understand the pattern, you can learn to stop the spitting. When spitting happens, there are two approaches you can take:

THE PLAYFUL APPROACH. Make it into a game. You could say, "That looks yummy! I think I'll put it on my hand to make my skin look shiny" (in an exaggerated performance).

THE LIMITING APPROACH. Set a gentle but firm limit that communicates this behavior is not okay. Move your body close to your child and say, "No. I can't let you spit on [me/your teacher/your friend/your sibling]. Come with me for few minutes. I'll stay with you until you feel better."

Build in time to connect, listen, hug, and reassure before each of the behavior patterns occurs. Then use one of the two approaches with your child. If crying or protests follow, continue to give your full attention to help the healing that follows after setting a limit.

Name-Calling

As a toddler develops speech and learns to talk, they might pick up negative terms or names as part of this process. When a child calls someone a negative name, it feels harsh to everyone involved—including your child. The words can feel hurtful, aggressive, abusive, insensitive, and insulting, and this can be triggering to parents. Before you react, pause and ask yourself these questions:

1. Where could have my child heard these words?

2. How do we handle conflict in our family?

3. What language do we use when we experience conflict in our family?

4. What kind of language is being used in the media that my child is watching?

STEP 4

If name-calling is a big trigger for you, pause and ask yourself these questions:

1. Did anyone call me names when I was a child? If yes, who was it and what names did they use?

2. Was there a caring adult to protect me from name-calling?

3. What is the earliest memory I have around this?

4. As an adult, what would I do for or say to that child who needed help but didn't get it?

5. As an adult, what would I do for or say to the person who called me names when I was a helpless child?

Getting in touch with these memories and emotions is the only way out of your inner prison. Spend some time alone or in the presence of another adult who can listen and help you intergrate these experiences from your past.

If name-calling has become a habitual attention-seeking behavior, you can do the following:

▸ Set a gentle but firm limit: Name-calling is not okay.
▸ Introduce humor to bring in laughter and connection. You can say, "Did someone call me a 'stupid head'? I can see my head, but I can't see my stupid. Hmm . . . where is the mirror? I need to check . . ." Encourage your toddler to laugh or giggle.
▸ Set aside some daily one-on-one time. Use it to do whatever your child wants. Let them take the lead; you will follow.

Talking Back

A toddler's language abilities are still fairly limited, which means that talking back is usually some variation of a firm and loud "NO! I don't want to!" or the occasional "You are stupid!"

Talking back can feel very triggering for a parent. Check in with yourself to see how you feel in the moment. Before you react, pause and ask yourself the following:

1. When does my toddler talk back?

2. What could my child *need* from me when talking back? Is it a limit, attention, play?

3. Have I been clear and consistent with setting limits, or do I break my own rules when I am tired and exhausted?

4. Could my toddler be working on some kind of fear or looking for an excuse to get my undivided attention?

If you feel triggered, walk away or breathe in deeply four to eight times to calm down and get back to the present moment.

If talking back has become a habitual attention-seeking behavior, you can do the following:

▸ Draw your body close to your child and establish eye-level contact. Place your arms on your child's arms. If they are holding something away from you, don't grab their hands. Let them hold whatever they need to.

▸ Set a gentle but firm limit by saying, "I can't let you unlock that door. It is not safe. I want to keep you safe. I'll stay here with you until you feel well enough to give me back the key."

‣ Introduce play to melt away tension and fear. You could role-play and say, "I need to wash the dishes, but I don't want to!" Then stomp your feet or throw yourself on the floor in a "tantrum." Most children will be fascinated by your silliness and will want to play along.

Play offers a safe and unthreatening invitation to have fun together. It will help your child come out of their "me-against-you" state of mind.

HOW TODDLERS TEST LIMITS

The self-determination theory states that human beings are driven in their behaviors and decisions by three psychological needs: the need for autonomy, the need for competence, and the need for relatedness.

A toddler's job is to test these limits. This is a healthy behavior that requires parents to be supportive and present. When toddlers use attention-seeking behaviors, they want to do the following:

- Break away from their parents (autonomy)

- Come up with their own rules (competence)

- Test if they are still loved and accepted (relatedness)

Children need rules, rituals, and structure. A parent's first job is to keep their child safe (physically and emotionally). This safety can be achieved by setting clear limits. This can be done in a gentle but firm way that makes a child feel safe and cared for. To do this, we must look within ourselves when faced with a toddler who talks back or breaks a rule in order to catch our reactive state (yelling, getting angry, withholding love, scolding, punishing).

HANDLING SOCIAL DIFFICULTIES

When we put ourselves in the mind of a toddler, we can see how overwhelming life can feel. There are so many new things to learn, infinite rules and schedules to abide, and very little control. This is hard on a young child, who needs constant reassurance that they are loved, cared for, and safe. With the addition of a sibling or being around another child, a toddler's life becomes even harder.

Jealousy

Jealousy is a common behavior in toddlers. It is natural for a toddler to feel jealous toward another child or a new baby sibling who demands our attention, even for a few minutes. When this happens, your child needs reassurance that they are seen and loved. It's unfair of us to expect our child to automatically love or accept the presence of another child who competes with them for our time and attention.

How can you embrace "jealousy" as a sign of parental attachment? Pay attention to your vocabulary. Do you find yourself using words such as "jealous," "selfish," or "needy" in response to your child seeking your attention? If so, ask yourself the following:

1. What is the need behind my child's behavior right now?

2. When was the last time I offered my child uninterrupted one-on-one time?

3. How often do I play with my toddler, and do I follow their lead in play?

4. Do I have developmentally inappropriate expectations for my toddler?

5. How much undivided attention did I receive from my parents when I was a child?

6. Did I feel "jealous" when I was a child? If so, was anyone there for me and when?

If jealousy begins to create social difficulties, you can do the following:

▹ Offer 5 to 10 minutes of daily uninterrupted one-on-one time.

▹ Play "I love you more!" games. Make a game of chase or tag into an "I love you more!" game. Bring a partner or family member into the game and "fight" for who gets to love your child the most.

▹ Be honest. Gently say, "I know this feels hard right now. I love you so much. I can't spend time with you this very moment, but we will have our 'you-and-me time' before bedtime. I promise. I can hold you now if you need to cry or feel sad."

Fighting

No child is born with the desire to fight or hurt another child. If your child has become overly aggressive, it means that they lack connection, attention, and affection. A child's healthy sense of self comes from feeling unconditionally accepted and loved. Responding to aggression with aggression does not work. Neither does rewarding "good behavior" as opposed to "bad."

Fighting and bullying are acts of physical aggression, and these are the signs of an angry child. An angry child is scared and needs our help to feel emotionally safe and connected. An aggressive child is . . .

- A scared and frightened child who feels isolated and alone.
- A child who feels fear inside their body.
- A child who does not have the cognitive ability to voice this fear and must act it out.
- A child who needs your help to reconnect.

If fighting begins to create social difficulties, you can do the following:

- Pay attention to your reaction first. If you lose your calm, walk away or rest for five minutes. Then come back to the present moment to address the need behind the behavior and not the behavior itself.
- Set a gentle but firm limit if your child is hurting you or another child.
- Make daily connection a priority in your relationship with your child. This should be 20 to 30 minutes of daily, uninterrupted one-on-one time. Plan to do this for the next three to six months. Slowly, changes will take place.
- Be playful. Get on the floor and wrestle or roughhouse. Let your toddler lead the play. Note that aggression against you may show up here. This is a good sign. Use it to set limits. Anticipate that hurt feelings may show up.
- Listen to your child's feelings. Let them cry. This is how your child heals fear.

For more tips on handling aggressive behavior, revisit **step 3**.

Resisting Relationships (Fear of Getting Close)

We are naturally drawn to other people. Close relationships within our social groups help develop a sense of belonging, which supports emotional, mental, and physical development.

Toddlers are innately social learners and connectors. They love to play and spend time with the adults, siblings, and friends in their lives. When a child doesn't follow this natural impulse to connect, it indicates a feeling of isolation and disconnection from the world around them. Their sense of personal boundaries may have been violated, and they are in a self-protection mode.

What are some cues that a child is resisting connection? They could . . .

- Not want to share a toy.
- Not want to hug or be hugged.
- Avoid making eye contact.
- Look lost.
- Cry or whine.
- Show disinterest in play and other activities.
- Insist on rigid behavior around food, sleep, play, or another parent.

These nonverbal cues are cries for help. When your child avoids connection, you can do the following:

- Examine triggers around your own rejection, to avoid reacting in the moment.

STEP 4

- Avoid forcing your toddler to be friendly or to hug or kiss someone (even another sibling). Doing so can violate a child's personal boundaries, which will deepen feelings of being unsafe and can intensify the fear of connection.
- Avoid using words such as "shy," "reserved," "fearful," "anxious," "afraid," or "introverted" when describing your child. These labels are not helpful.
- If another adult questions or criticizes your child's behavior (especially in front of your toddler), politely thank the person for their observation and walk away. Tell your child that you love them, right then and there.

If your child's behavior is criticized or questioned, use this as an opportunity instead to question your unconscious beliefs around being accepted for who you are, the need to please others, and what it feels like to not have your own voice be heard.

SHOWING AND
TEACHING EMPATHY

Children maintain a sense of connection and belonging from their daily interactions with parents and other caretakers. When parents show unconditional love and empathy, children learn to love and be empathic toward others. Yet this empathic connection can easily break down.

Your responses can teach your toddler their place in the world and can help shape their sense of self. To model empathy, you can do the following:

▸ Teach your child simple language to communicate feelings: "I see that you feel frustrated that you can't play with the truck right now. It's hard to wait, isn't it? I'll stay with you while you wait."

▸ Model empathy in the adult relationships that your child observes daily. For example, if your partner has a bad day, you can model empathy by giving them a hug.

▸ Use storytelling to talk about feelings. When reading together, you can ask: "The tiger was lost. I wonder how the tiger was feeling. What do you think?"

▸ Be honest with your child about your feelings, especially when they ask you directly. If they ask whether you're upset, you can say, "Yes, I feel really sad right now. Thank you for caring. I love you."

MANTRA

*My child and I have a precious emotional bond
that requires daily nurturing and attention.
I commit to paying attention to how I feel
when I am triggered. I am grateful to my toddler
for showing me where I need to grow.*

STEP 4 RECAP

1. Emotional safety is the result of a child's integrated state of the reptilian brain, limbic system, and prefrontal cortex.

2. Behavior is driven by need, and parents must understand the need behind the behavior.

3. Connection before correction.

4. Parents can listen well and be playful.

5. Words are powerful. We must be conscious of the labels we use when talking about our children.

REFLECTION QUESTIONS

1. How can I educate myself about my child's emotions so that I can have a better understanding and more empathy?

2. What are my limiting beliefs around social acceptance and/or putting my needs first?

3. Are there disempowering words or labels that I can eliminate from my vocabulary?

4. How can I model empathy toward myself in order to teach my child?

5. What can I learn about the cause-and-effect relationship between needs and behavior in my child?

STAY CONNECTED

Conscious parenting is a journey of personal growth. Part of it is learning how to stay connected—to our children, our families, our communities, and one another. Staying connected requires personal growth both as a parent and an ever-evolving individual, as well as a vision for our family and our life. Fortunately, toddlers are the best teachers on this journey. They will generously create endless opportunities to "look in the mirror" every single day.

In order to stay connected to your child, a culture of connection must be the foundation of your family. In this chapter, you'll learn how to foster self-awareness and prioritize connection with yourself, in your relationships with others, and with your environment outside the home. Each opportunity for connection is one step on the path toward becoming a conscious parent.

MINDFULNESS AND SELF-CARE

Awareness of our thoughts and feelings takes practice and a strong commitment. There's a natural tendency to automatically revert to old thinking patterns and unquestioned reactions that we have used in the past to self-protect. In relationships with our children, some default reactions may be yelling, giving orders, rewarding or punishing, withholding affection, over-planning and over-scheduling, using labels like "good" and "bad," or grabbing your child.

There are mindful practices that you can integrate into your daily life that will help you self-regulate when parenting feels overwhelming.

SELF-CHECK

When we take care of ourselves, our minds and hearts stay attuned to our toddler's needs and will lead to less reactivity on our part. If you have trouble establishing a self-care practice, refer back to "The Importance of Self-Care" in **step 1**.

Mindful Practice #1: Conscious Breathing

Our modern lives are busy, and it often feels as if there's not enough time to pause, take a breath, and recover from stressful moments, which for parents never seem to end.

Conscious breathing helps us "come back" to our bodies and into the present moment. Focusing on slowly breathing in and out calms our nervous system and helps us be less reactive, more present, and attuned to our child's need in the moment.

This practice takes only a minute and is easy to do. Start by inhaling one full breath and filling your lungs; then slowly exhale to a count of five. You can make a soft exhaling sound if that feels good. Repeat these steps five or six times.

Mindful Practice #2: Gratitude and Self-Compassion

Gratitude and self-compassion are important elements of conscious parenting. When we practice both, we remind ourselves that we are safe and worthy of living a beautiful life.

When we feel triggered, we often react because we feel threatened in some way. Regardless of whether the threat is real or in our head, the fear response will automatically kick in. Gratitude and fear cannot coexist.

To counter fear-based triggers, practice gratitude and self-compassion by doing the following:

- Keep a gratitude journal and write in it daily, either when you wake up or before you go to bed. This sets the tone for the next day.
- Write down 10 things that you feel grateful for, small or big, each day. Be sure to include at least three feelings of gratitude toward yourself.
- Create a mantra of self-compassion and say it aloud when you finish your daily gratitude practice. Consider looking at yourself in the mirror and making eye contact as you repeat your mantra. It can help soften your self-judgments.

Mindful Practice #3: Notice Your Triggers

Our childhood experiences shaped us into the adults we are today. When there are painful, unresolved childhood experiences from the past, these can trigger unconscious self-protecting behaviors in our parenting.

How can you learn to catch these behaviors before they get triggered?

- For 30 days, commit to noticing of all of your triggers (emotional and mental).
- Pay attention to your triggers throughout each day.
- When you feel triggered, write it down in a notebook that you keep with you.
- After 30 days, spend some time alone to read all the triggers that you recorded.

Now ask yourself these questions:

- What is it that stands out to me?
- What reactive behaviors are occurring on a daily basis?
- Is there a pattern in my emotional reactivity?
- Is there a pattern in my mental reactivity?

Whatever comes up for you, start there and treat it with an abundance of self-compassion.

CONNECTING WITHIN

Discovering, connecting, and nurturing our inner selves is the foundational work of conscious parenting. To make your inner self a constant presence in your mind and heart, try the following techniques:

- Find a photo of yourself as a young child and display it somewhere you'll see every day. Choose the age that speaks to you the most.

- When you feel overwhelmed by parenting or other circumstances in your life, stop to look at this photo.

- Pause and take a moment to breathe slowly in and out.

- Close your eyes. Picture yourself as a child and ask, "What do you need right now?"

- Accept and embrace the answer, whatever it is, and then act on this need.

- Make this need a priority in your life.

Self-Care Practice #1: Sleep, Nutrition, and Exercise

Our mindfulness and self-awareness depend on our relationship with our bodies. This marvelous and complex human system is designed to keep us healthy and alive, but it needs adequate sleep, nutritious food, and plenty of physical movement to thrive. Ask yourself the following:

- ▸ Do you feel at home in your own body?
- ▸ Are you listening to your body?
- ▸ Are you honoring your body's needs?
- ▸ Do you have a love/hate relationship with your body?

If your answers are negative, and you don't know where to start, you are not alone. These guidelines can help:

- ▸ Give your body seven to eight hours of restorative sleep a night.
- ▸ Feed your body nutritious, whole foods. (Avoid refined sugar and processed foods.)
- ▸ Move your body every day, even if it's just a 20-minute walk.
- ▸ Find a sport that you love, such as biking or kickboxing. Commit to practicing it at least two or three times per week.

Use these guidelines as an opportunity to educate yourself. Experiment with new foods and different types of physical exercise. Make this a learning experience filled with surprise and self-discovery.

Self-Care Practice #2: Listen

Parents make time for their children when strong emotions arise, but who makes time for Mom or Dad? As a conscious parent, you need to create a safe and healing space to work through your emotions, worries, and past hurts. You need to be listened to, felt, heard, seen, and fully embraced by another adult. It is a responsibility to yourself and your child.

You can do this by integrating a time for listening as a self-care practice. This can be time with a therapist or a close friend but should not be a spouse, partner, or immediate family member. Emotional safety is the premise of this exchange.

If you want to spend time with a friend, it's important that you listen and not just speak. Be sure to do the following:

- Establish a predetermined amount of time each week.
- Take turns listening to each other. Don't offer advice, interrupt, or validate anything being said.
- When you are the listener, offer your full love and attention to the speaker.
- When you are the speaker, remember that you are safe; allow access to deep-seated hurts, and bring that pain to surface.
- Either of you may cry, sob, tremble, shake, or laugh. This is your body releasing old emotional hurts, and it supports the connection with your inner child.

If you can afford therapy, find a therapist who is trained to listen well. Start with a few sessions and see where they take you. Stay open and nonjudgmental to what you will uncover.

Self-Care Practice #3: Meditation

Meditation and mindfulness are ways that we can practice awareness and develop skills to remain calm in the heat of the moment. The benefits of meditation include decreased levels of anxiety, depression, and stress, as well as increased levels of concentration, emotional well-being, and gratitude. Still, busy parents may find it difficult to build a regular meditation practice, especially if mindfulness is new to them. Fortunately, there are many ways to meditate:

- Find a quiet corner or place inside your home where you can sit quietly to meditate.
- Start small. Try meditating for just five minutes every day. Then, as you become more comfortable, slowly increase the time.

- Try listening to a guided meditation. Use an app such as Headspace or Calm.
- Listen to music that inspires meditation or play music in the background during a quiet part of the day.
- Take a yoga class that includes a meditation practice.

JOURNALING

Keeping a daily journal can help us reconnect with our deeper self. In this safe space, we can write down everything we think and feel. As we give voice to our needs, fears, and desires, we become detached from them and they no longer control us.

When journaling, take note of whatever surfaces, and use this to honor your needs. This can be a deeply healing and emotional process that offers new perspectives and insights. It can be used to enhance a meditation practice or even as a precursor to meditation.

CULTIVATING CONSCIOUS RELATIONSHIPS

Relationships are the engines of our personal growth and evolution. Each person in our life mirrors an aspect of ourselves that requires reflection. These are the people who challenge our unconscious beliefs or who model conscious behavior that we feel encouraged to follow. Welcoming this "reflection" helps us uncover the self-limiting beliefs that hold us back and pave the positive way forward.

Cultivating conscious relationships improves the quality of our lives and can give your child a model to follow. What does a conscious relationship with a partner, a family member, or with someone within your community look like? How can you apply the principles of conscious parenting to the significant relationships in your life?

In your relationships with others, seek to do the following:

Step 1: Find calm

Step 2: Understand their behavior

Step 3: Establish a feeling of safety

Step 4: Connect emotionally

Let's examine more closely the relationships that you, as a parent, may have with the people in your life—a spouse or partner, your immediate family, and your greater community. Use the guided reflection questions as prompts to help you think about the quality of the most significant relationships in your life. Pay attention to sensations of openness or resistance and consider what you need to feel loved and supported.

Parents, Spouses, and Partners

A romantic partner is a source of emotional connection that requires you to love and accept them for who they are and to be honest with them about who you are, what you need, and what you want. This can make us feel quite vulnerable at times. It requires us to feel safe and to ensure that our partner feels the same way in return.

To establish a feeling of safety, it's important to show affection and commitment on a daily basis. Ensure that you have time together, alone and without any kids. In your conversations, express curiosity about their emotional and mental world and empathy for their inner experience. Just as you might have rituals with your child, create rituals with your partner—something just for the two of you.

Reflection questions:

1. Am I trying to change them to fit my ideal vision of a partner?

2. Do I feel safe to express my feelings and what I need?

3. Do they feel safe to express how they feel and what they need?

4. Do I judge my partner?

5. Are we on the same page as parents?

6. Are we mindful about how we handle conflict?

Co-parenting

A co-parenting relationship is the mutual agreement between two separated, divorced, or unmarried parents of the same child or children. This relationship may be difficult, filled with resentment and prone to conflict, or it may be harmonious, one in which both parents make the health and safety of their child a priority.

If your co-parenting relationship is a difficult one, try to shift your perspective to one of gratitude. You can be grateful for the wonderful child or children that you now share and thankful that a former partner showed you what you do not want in your life. If you need to grieve the relationship, then give yourself time to do so and help your child move through any pain or loss that they may experience.

Regardless of whether your co-parenting relationship is smooth and easy or fraught with discord, the only parent that you have control over in this relationship is *you*. Your co-parent will have feelings that you cannot control, and your child will have feelings about their family situation and their other parent.

> The only parent that you have control over in any relationship is you.

Young children who are raised with co-parents may have big feelings like anger, resentment, hate, or jealousy. In order to navigate these difficult emotions, a child needs a shame- and guilt-free environment and for those around them to have empathy for how they feel. As a co-parent, you can incorporate lots of play, time to listen or be present for their emotions, and ways to honor their needs. These are your go-to strategies.

Reflection questions:

1. Do I show my child's co-parent respect as a human being?

2. Do I have empathy for their inner pain, whether expressed or hidden?

3. Did we agree on a parenting plan that works for both of us?

4. Am I conscious about how I talk about the other parent to my child?

5. Am I releasing the need for control about how the co-parent is raising our child?

6. Am I fully aware that the only control I have is of myself and the relationship I build with my child?

CO-PARENTING WITH CONSCIOUSNESS

Co-parenting demands a lot of us because at the heart of the relationship is a child who loves both parents equally. Your own feelings toward your former partner may range from anger and jealousy to disappointment and sadness.

Here are some tips for how to start co-parenting with consciousness:

1. Let children know that both parents love them unconditionally.

2. Avoid making negative comments about the other parent in front of your child.

3. Resolve conflicts and disagreements when your child is not present.

4. Avoid letting your child act as a mediator or messenger from one parent to the other.

5. When you feel overwhelmed, be honest with yourself and with your child. Reassure your child that you will be able to handle the situation.

6. Work with a listening partner or a therapist to release any negative feelings so that they do not affect your relationship with your child.

If you've already made some mistakes, have compassion for yourself. Then start over. Every day is a new opportunity to make conscious choices when co-parenting.

Family

Human beings are complex. It makes sense that our relationships with others are equally complex. When those people are part of your family, balancing the need for connection with competing self-interests and conflicting beliefs can feel like navigating a minefield.

It's helpful to remember that conscious relationships with our family members begin with us. It starts with becoming self-aware and knowing what our boundaries are. And it requires being vulnerable yet feeling safe enough to express those boundaries and needs to a parent, an in-law, or an older sibling. However, it is necessary if we want our family members to have a meaningful presence in our life and that of our child.

Use empathy-based communication to express what you need and expect from your family and to accept them in return.

Reflection questions:

1. Can I accept my family members for who they are without attempting to change or control them?

2. Am I honoring my boundaries and theirs?

3. Am I honest with them? Do I mean what I say?

4. Am I putting my fear of acceptance ahead of my need to be authentic?

5. Did we agree on protocols for asking for help from each other?

6. Do I show my appreciation for them regularly?

Blended Families

A blended family includes a committed couple and the children from either parent's previous marriages, relationships, or adoptions. The relationships in a blended family can be quite complex, more so than many may realize at first. There can be multiple agents in the roles of biological parent, stepparent, and co-parent, as well as biological children, stepchildren, and stepsiblings.

When things go well, a blended family can be a wonderful experience. Children benefit from the richness of new relationships in their life. However, "blending" does not happen overnight. As new family members enter the relationship, new dynamics arise and new sensitivities are introduced. Children may need consistent and substantial emotional support as they adjust to a new family life.

If you are considering entering into a blended family, or creating one, take some time to check in with yourself and make sure you feel prepared for this change. Check in with your partner and discuss whether they are ready to become a stepparent, particularly if they don't have children of their own.

Reflection questions:

1. Am I clear with my partner about my co-parenting needs, schedule, priorities, and financial implications?

2. Is my partner clear with me about their co-parenting needs, schedule, priorities, and financial implications?

3. Do my partner and I agree about living arrangements, the financial impact of blending our families, personal financial responsibilities, and how to maintain a work-life balance?

4. Is my child ready for a new family? Am I consciously helping my child transition to this change?

5. Am I allowing my child to safely express emotions of hurt or rejection at the idea of a new partner and/or stepsiblings?

Community

Having a sense of community and belonging can make us feel that we matter, that we have a bigger purpose in life. A community can be as small as three or four individuals or as big as a town or city. It can even be a virtual community, where strangers engage and interact online. Being part of a community offers us an opportunity to make a difference in other people's lives and gives meaning and fulfillment to our own.

You may already be part of an established community, a place where you can reach out for support and offer it in return. Those looking to join or build a community can create one around common interests or join a larger community whose interests you already share. Your active role in a community will model for your child the importance of human connection and shared experiences. Children learn that they are not alone and that human beings are interdependent.

Reflection questions:

1. Do I feel connected to the world around me?

2. Do I meet or share life experiences with like-minded people?

3. Am I following my passion?

4. Do I feel that I contribute to my community in any way?

5. What can I give without expecting anything in return?

Parenting Support System

Parenting is hard and all parents need support, which allows them to show up present and open, full of empathy for their children. A support system may include your partner or loved one, several family members, and even a babysitter. Consider extending outside this immediate circle and allow your support system to embrace close and trusted friends, neighbors, your listening partner or mentor, and a larger parent support group.

Reflection questions:

1. Do I belong to a parent support group or something similar?

2. Do I have a weekly exchange of listening time with another parent?

3. Do I have an emergency list of contacts to call at any time of day or night?

4. Do I have a neighbor to reach out to in case of an emergency?

5. Do other parents know about and share my struggles?

CREATE A NURTURING ENVIRONMENT

Your relationships expand beyond your immediate family and can impact both you and your child. Although you can't control how other people behave, think, or feel, you can control your choices in creating a nurturing environment when choosing your external support system.

Childcare

Leaving our child in the care of others can trigger anxiety, doubt, and concern. Is there a way to ensure that the principles of conscious parenting extend outside the home and into a place where our toddler will spend much of their day?

There are values you can look for when considering off-site care for your child. Look for teachers who are trained to deal with difficult emotions and to use language consciously. Consider how your toddler will feel here and if they will be allowed to express themselves without judgment. Will your toddler feel safe, seen, heard, and valued?

Reflection questions:

1. Am I making myself available to the teachers to listen, help, and volunteer?

2. Am I open to learn from the teachers?

3. Do I show respect and appreciation for the work that teachers do every day?

4. Do I have a good rapport with the other parents in the class?

5. Do I support the school's projects and initiatives to the best of my abilities?

The Working Parent

Many working parents spend an average of 40 hours or more per week away from their child. Since this is where we might spend most of our time, where we work matters to our overall well-being and quality of life. We desire work with organizations that share our values around parenting and family. We want to feel supported and appreciated by our co-workers or supervisors. We should feel safe to request time off or to coordinate remote working arrangements if our child needs us to be home. And as people, we want to be valued as creative individuals who contribute to the greater good through our work. The result is a feeling of accomplishment that feeds our energy and supports a positive relationship with our child and others.

Reflection questions:

1. Do I take time off when I need it?

2. Can I make arrangements to work remotely, at least partially?

3. Do I work overtime even though I can leave on time? Why?

4. Do I feel motivated to come to work every day?

5. Do I feel that I make a contribution in the world through my work? If not, can I change my job or means of income?

The Stay-at-Home Parent

The parent who stays home or works from home to help raise a child while another parent leaves for work still needs to feel valued in order to maintain connection and harmony within the relationship. Make time for open and honest conversations with your partner about this arrangement—how long it will last, each partner's duties and responsibilities, the financial implications of this decision, and the freedom to change it.

It's important that the stay-at-home parent does not feel that this decision is forced on them. A parent who does not enjoy this role or feels undervalued in it risks feelings of aggression, resentment, or blame toward their partner and even their child.

Reflection questions:

1. Do I feel valued and appreciated for the work that I do?

2. Do I plan for time alone or time outside the home without the children?

3. Do I feel guilt or shame for not bringing more money home?

4. Is my partner supportive of my decision to be a stay-home parent?

5. Do I value my contribution as a parent or do I need constant validation from my partner and others?

6. Do I believe that I need to self-sacrifice? If so, how can I change this unconscious belief?

MAINTAINING A GROWTH MINDSET

Cultivating a growth mindset means focusing on effort and progress rather than outcome. This can be learned at any age.

To cultivate a growth mindset in your family, try the following:

- Praise effort and learning over results. Instead of saying "You are so smart" or "You are so good," say, "I can see how much effort you've put into this project."

- See progress as growth, even when it is small.

- Avoid viewing the world around you as dualistic (good/bad, right/wrong).

- There is no failure and there are no mistakes—only growth.

MANTRA

*I cannot control or change my child.
I cannot control or change anyone other
than myself. I have power over what
I choose to do with my own feelings.*

*I have the power to shift my consciousness by
letting go of my old beliefs and identities.*

STEP 5 RECAP

1. Staying connected requires commitment and practice.

2. Our environment creates our world. We have the ability to nurture our environments in our workplace, our childcare choices, and at home through mindfulness, self-care, and a growth mindset.

3. There are no mistakes, only learning, as long as we look for the lessons.

4. The quality of our relationships determines the quality of our lives.

5. The only person we have control over is ourselves.

REFLECTION QUESTIONS

1. Am I oriented toward growth and learning?

2. What holds me back from developing a growth mindset? Is it self-judgment, shame, or guilt? What kind of work do I need to do to change my mindset?

3. How do I show up in my close relationships?

4. Do relationships matter to me? Why or why not?

5. How do I model self-awareness for my child?

Part Two

CONSCIOUS PARENTING IN ACTION

In Part One, you walked step-by-step through the principles of conscious parenting. You learned to find calm in the heat of the moment, to understand your toddler's behavior, how to establish a feeling of safety, how to connect emotionally, and how to stay connected with others.

In Part Two we'll focus on the practical tools and immediate solutions to challenges typical to toddlerhood. Part Two can then be used in the heat of the moment. As soon as you realize that you are reacting from autopilot rather than mindful presence, skip ahead to Part Two for immediate support.

COMMON BEHAVIORS AND CONFLICTS

It's one thing to understand the principle behind "finding calm," but quite another to practice it in the midst of your toddler throwing a temper tantrum in the grocery store aisle. Part Two puts the principles of conscious parenting into practice. Here you'll find brief advice for what to do in the moment and the steps to use when encountering some of the most common behaviors and conflicts during the toddler years. Use this section to help you remember how to practice step 3 when your toddler is whining or how step 4 can guide you if your toddler refuses to share.

TANTRUMS

A tantrum is a seemingly "irrational" behavior such as screaming, crying, yelling, and throwing oneself on the floor.

Why It's Happening

Toddlers have tamper tantrums when they cannot cope with the frustration from having limits imposed upon them by an adult (being told "no," adhering to a bedtime, or being told to brush their teeth) or when they are unable to achieve a goal (not being able to walk or tie their shoelaces).

What to Do

Accept that a toddler cannot think rationally while in the middle of a tantrum. Remember to find calm (STEP 1) and try to understand that what your toddler needs (STEP 2) is to feel validated, seen, and safe.

How to Act

To help your toddler feel safe, start by lowering yourself so that you are at eye level with your child. Then do the following:

1. Set a gentle but firm limit (**STEP 3**), especially if someone's physical safety is at risk.

2. Listen, listen, listen. This is a chance to connect emotionally through the healing power of listening (**STEP 4**).

3. Validate your child's feelings using short, matter-of-fact statements. Say, "I can see why you feel frustrated right now." Avoid telling them to stop crying or to stop their behavior.

4. Maintain eye contact and gently touch your child if they allow it, but avoid forcing a hug or kiss.

5. Softly say, "I am here. You are safe. I am sorry this is so hard right now. I love you."

Teaching Moment

A strong need for autonomy drives most toddler behavior. This desire to be independent from the parent is a part of their development and should be encouraged. When there are rules or restrictions that hamper their independence, a toddler's high level of frustration may trigger a tantrum.

In the face of a tantrum, you may feel triggered, overwhelmed by feelings of anger, powerless, or embarrassed. Ask yourself:

- When did I feel this way as a child?
- What is my earliest memory when I felt this way?
- What did I need as a child when I felt this way?

TRY THIS INSTEAD

Remember that your toddler needs you right now. If your child is having trouble self-regulating, stay connected (**step 5**). Breathe consciously and invite your child to breathe with you. If they don't follow your example in the moment, then trust that they will remember another time. Continue to stay present, offer warmth, and make eye contact.

WHINING

Whining means that your toddler feels lost, helpless, and confused. This is their way of asking for help to get un-stuck because they cannot get out of this state on their own.

Why It's Happening

Toddlers are driven by a strong need to explore the world in order to discover their own preferences, desires, and uniqueness. A toddler will use whining as a vehicle to off-load feelings of desperation, helplessness, frustration, or even fear.

What to Do

Remain calm (STEP 1). Be an anchor for your child in this difficult moment and prepare to hold that safe space for as long as needed (STEP 3). Remember that your toddler is not trying to manipulate you; they are asking for your help.

How to Act

1. Lower yourself so that you are at eye level with your child; you can even lie down on the floor.

2. Make eye contact.

3. Softly say, "I am here. I know this feels hard right now for you. I will stay with you for as long as you need."

Teaching Moment

Staying present with a whining toddler is not easy. Consider this an opportunity to practice patience and compassion and to give your young child abundant attention and affection.

If you find yourself triggered by feelings of impatience or a lack of empathy for your child's experience in this moment, reflect on these questions:

- Why is it hard for me to show empathy to my whining child?
- What could block me from showing my unconditional love in this moment?
- Was I treated with patience and empathy when I was a child?

NONCOMPLIANCE (OPPOSITIONAL BEHAVIORS)

Noncompliance, or oppositional behavior, includes running away and hiding or ignoring the adult. This behavior comes from a toddler's strong need for self-discovery, autonomy, and independence. Oppositional behaviors are neither good nor bad; they are a natural development of the toddler becoming a separate being from the parent (STEP 2). The parent's role is to set clear and loving limits as often as needed.

Why It's Happening

Toddlers use oppositional behavior to understand their world and to test the limits of that world as imposed by parents and society. The toddler needs to make personal choices and to feel in control of their life.

What to Do

Allow your child to oppose you while still making sure they are safe (STEP 3). If this limit leads to crying, allow the child to cry for as long as necessary. Avoid telling your child not to cry—just let it happen. Try to reestablish connection through listening or play. Wrestle or tumble on the floor, have a pillow fight or throw soft toys—anything that will get you both laughing. Laughter will help your child trust you again and feel seen.

How to Act

1. Make eye contact with your child.

2. Offer your arms for a hug or a lap so that they can be held. If your child rejects these signs of affection, accept this as normal. They are testing whether you are really on their "side."

3. Prepare to listen to feelings of anger, disappointment, and frustration.

4. Validate those feelings in short, neutral statements. Say, "I can see you feel disappointed. Feeling the way you feel right now is very normal."

5. Reconnect by saying, "I am here with you for as long as you need to feel better." You can also reconnect through play. Ask, "How about we throw socks at each other?"

Teaching Moment

Self-regulation can be difficult for parents when a child doesn't follow instruction. Try not to take this defiance personally. If you feel triggered to react as a means of self-protection, consider this an opportunity to reflect on your relationship to authority and control (STEP 1). Reflect on these questions:

- Why do I need to be "right" in this moment?
- Why is it hard for me to accept this defiance as a neutral behavior?
- How was I treated as a child when I didn't comply?

TRY THIS INSTEAD

If your child can be safe without you, walk away for few minutes. Anchor yourself to the present moment. Close your eyes and breathe deeply. Inhale for a count of four and exhale for a count of five. Do this at least six times. Recognize that you don't have to figure out anything right now. Return and be present with your child, continue to offer warmth and maintain eye contact.

REFUSING TO SHARE

Toddlers want to play with other children as a way to learn new things and to bond socially. Refusing to share (be it a toy, snack, parent, or teacher) arises when a toddler loses their sense of connection and safety.

Why It's Happening

Refusing to share may look like rigid and "selfish" behavior, but it is a cry for help. Your toddler wants to feel safe and connected and is using this behavior to communicate their need for your attention.

What to Do

When your toddler refuses to share, it is because they feel disconnected—from friends, siblings, and parents. They are not thinking clearly in this moment, and lecturing or scolding them will only increase their existing pain. You are the only person who can help your child recover a sense of belonging and social connection (STEP 4).

Mentally prepare yourself to show empathy and patience. Avoid asking for the truth, as it is irrelevant. Whatever your child is feeling is true for them. Validate their feelings and listen. Understand there may by an emotional release, such as crying, trembling, or anger (STEP 3).

Momentarily put on hold any chores or plans.

How to Act

1. Stay calm (STEP 1).

2. Lower yourself to eye level with your child and make eye contact.

3. Attempt a gentle touch, if they allow it.

4. Invite them to tell you what happened. Say, "I see you are having a hard time right now. Tell me what is going on. I want to listen. I am here for you." Listen without interruption.

5. If your toddler is still learning to talk, use your body language by inviting them into your open arms. It's okay if they run away from you.

Teaching Moment

Refusing to share can be a thorny trigger for many parents. We want to raise our children to be good-hearted. Use this trigger as a teaching moment to become more aware of any pain around "belonging" and any personal boundaries within a social group.

Reflect on these questions:

- Did I have siblings or friends who didn't share with me? If yes, how did I feel? Did anyone help me cope with the situation?
- Was I ever forced to share something of mine against my will?
- As an adult today, am I clear with others about my personal boundaries?

TRY THIS INSTEAD

If your child's refusal to share means that you can't be loving, then walk away for a few minutes. Repeat your self-compassion mantra three times (**step 5**). Trust that another opportunity to defuse your trigger will appear soon.

LYING

Lying is the intentional act of hiding or manipulating the truth to benefit oneself. While this may be true for an adult, a child between the ages of one and three years old does not yet have the cognitive ability to lie with intent. So what is happening when you catch your child in a lie?

Why It's Happening

When a toddler lies, this is an attempt to the test limits of a parent's love. For example, your three-year-old pulls the cans from a cabinet and onto the floor. When you ask who did this, your toddler might say, "I don't know . . . I think the cat/dog/brother/sister/imaginary friend did it." They may lie to avoid punishment and to preserve your love.

What to Do

Your toddler may lack the cognitive ability to lie or manipulate you, but, as a parent, you can be a role model of honesty and truth by never lying to your child (not even "white" lies). This will prove to your child that you are someone who can be trusted at all times (STEP 4).

How to Act

Avoid interrogation-like questions or accusations of wrongdoing that might guilt or shame.

1. Stay neutral. Treat the lie as if your toddler had just told you a story.
2. Guide your toddler into the truth. Say, "I see that all of our cans are on the floor. I bet you were curious to see what was in there. What did you find? (Listen or allow for silence). "I am going to help you put them all back one by one. Here comes the first one."

Teaching Moment

Lying is an opportunity for a parent's personal healing and growth. If being lied to is a trigger for you, consider this an invitation to heal your wounds around betrayal and trust. Doing so will enable you to handle this situation with mindfulness.

Start by paying attention to how you feel in your body. Locate any sensations of discomfort and make a mental note of them. During meditation or while journaling, reflect on these questions:

- Who lied to me or betrayed me as a child?
- Who is my child reminding me of when they lie to me?
- What did I wish I could have done or said (but couldn't) to the adults who betrayed me?

The sooner you heal this wound, the stronger your relationship with your child will be.

TRY THIS INSTEAD

If you catch yourself in a lie (STEP 5) in your adult relationships with your partner, at work, with your friends, or your parents, ask yourself why you lied and what stops you from speaking your truth. Remember, you cannot stay connected with your child if you do not remain self-aware.

DISRESPECT AND AGGRESSION

Behavior that is labeled "disrespectful" includes talking back, name-calling, rudeness, interrupting, throwing things, mocking others, and not following instructions. We consider this behavior aggressive when it includes biting, kicking, pulling hair, destroying things, fighting, scratching, and stomping.

Why It's Happening

A toddler's primary communication is their behavior. A disrespectful or an aggressive child is scared and can't think well in the moment. Their sense of safety and connection is fleeting and can easily break down. Acting in disruptive ways is how they tell us that they need love and attention. We must reconnect with them—again and again, multiple times a day.

What to Do

A toddler who is being disrespectful or aggressive is seeking your loving attention (STEP 1); it means there is an immediate need to reconnect with you (STEP 4). Assess the situation and identify what your toddler needs in the moment: physical safety, emotional connection, food, sleep, or soothing touch. Cater to that need first. Next, validate their feelings in a gentle and neutral tone; whatever your child is feeling is true for them. Avoid using labels such as "bad behavior" so that your toddler won't internalize a message that *they* are bad.

How to Act

1. Stay calm (STEP 1).

2. Listen to your child's feelings without judgment or interruption (STEPS 3 and 4). Your child's behavior is their way of releasing painful emotions that they can't understand.

3. Make eye contact and, using physical closeness, set a gentle but firm limit on their behavior.

4. Use play to reconnect with your child and help them release the fear or pain causing the behavior through laughter or crying (which is also a positive outcome of creating a sense of safety for your child).

Teaching Moment

Don't feel defeated by how much attention your toddler needs. You are not alone and most parents feel this way during the toddler years. Adopt mindfulness and self-care practices (STEP 5) to remind yourself that self-compassion and empathy are skills learned with time and repetition.

If you feel triggered by your toddler's aggression and disrespect, consider this an opportunity to heal unresolved trauma from your past. Reflect on these questions:

- Who does my child remind me of when they act this way?
- As a child, did I witness aggression, conflict, and disrespect?
- As a child, was I the recipient of aggressive behavior?
- As a child, how did I feel in the presence of aggression?
- Was there anyone there to protect me?
- If I could go back in time, what would I do for or say to myself as a child?

TRY THIS INSTEAD

Accept that parenting is hard. If you lose your temper with your child, apologize and explain what happened and why. Say, "I am sorry I yelled earlier. You must have felt so scared when I yelled. I didn't mean to do that. You did nothing wrong. I will listen to you better next time."

JEALOUSY

Jealousy is common and is natural in young children. Feeling jealous teaches the child that they can't have something (a parent's attention or a toy) that they want in the moment.

Why It's Happening

A toddler may feel jealous if they perceive that their emotional connection with a parent is threatened, either by another child or someone else. A toddler will not understand rational explanations of why they should love, say, a younger brother or sister, and trying to explain this will only deepen their feeling of disconnection and isolation. They might think: "*I* am alone! Nobody understands me! My mommy/daddy only loves my baby sister/brother now."

What to Do

Accept jealousy as a natural and neutral feeling. Avoid attaching negative connotations to the word "jealous" or labeling a child as such. Allow your child to express their feeling however they choose, whether it's crying, getting angry, or throwing a tantrum.

Jealousy is asking for reassurance of a parent's love. Schedule 10 to 15 minutes of one-on-one time with your child (STEP 5) every day, just the two of you. During this time, let them lead any play time. This daily practice will rebuild your emotional connection, a resource that they can draw on in the future when they feel jealous.

How to Act

1. Remain calm (STEP 1).

2. Lower your body so that you are at eye level with
   your child.

3. Say, "I love you very much. I understand how hard this
   is for you."

4. Listen to their feelings. If you find that you can't
   listen well, tell your child, "I am sorry I can't listen
   to you right now. I love you very much. You are so
   important to me. I promise I will listen to you later
   before bedtime."

5. Offer lots of smiles, touch, and your warm presence.

Teaching Moment

Jealousy can be a cause of tension in adult relationships. If your
toddler's jealousy triggers you, become aware of any old wounds
and integrate them. This awareness may be enough for you to
avoid reacting toward your child during these times.

Reflect on these questions:

▸ How do I feel when my child show signs of jealousy?
▸ What is the earliest memory I have of feeling this way?
  How old was I?
▸ What do I need when my child is feeling jealous?

LACK OF IMPULSE CONTROL

A lack of impulse control is the result of an overwhelming emotional state. When a toddler feels overwhelmed by their environment or emotions, their executive functions (cognition, reason, logic, abstract thinking, and self-regulation) shut down. Without these active functions, a child cannot think rationally in the moment.

Why It's Happening

Children act irrationally (i.e., lose control of their impulse) when they are scared, fearful, or in emotional pain. Behind any unpleasant behavior is an unmet need. Irrational behavior (anger, temper tantrums, aggressive behavior, withdrawing, clinginess, etc.) is how children communicate feelings of fear and disconnection that need a parent's immediate attention.

What to Do

Children are wired for connection. If your child lost a sense of emotional safety and connection, their lack of impulse control is telling you that they need your help (**STEP 4**). Stay calm and present to your child's need in the moment.

How to Act

Create emotional safety and show empathy through your warm and loving presence.

1. Get close to your child and set a firm but gentle limit by holding the hand that is ready to hit or throw a toy.

2. Make eye contact and calmly say, "I can't let you hurt me or anyone else. I know this is hard for you right now. I'll stay here with you."

3. If your child allows it, touch them. If not, stay close nonetheless.

4. Validate what your child is feeling in the moment. Repeat, "I am here with you. You are safe now. I love you."

5. Listen to your child, even as they cry, scream, rage, or tremble.

6. If you feel inspired to, propose a game. Don't be afraid to experiment.

Teaching Moment

A lack of impulse control reminds us that we are still learning self-regulation, even as adults. Consider this an invitation to be vulnerable, honest, and transparent with ourselves and with our children. Reflect on these questions:

- How do I model self-regulation and impulse control for my child?
- Do I apologize to my child when I lose my temper?
- Are my expectations of my child realistic and age appropriate?

TRY THIS INSTEAD

Keep a daily journal. Start your day remembering that you are a good parent who is healing and growing your awareness one day at a time. Write down your thoughts and feelings whenever you feel triggered by your child's irrational behavior. Repeat your self-compassion mantra regularly.

CHALLENGES AROUND FOOD

Early on, toddlers show preferences for certain foods, and this is normal. If a parent tries to impose their beliefs about food onto a young child, this can result in a power struggle between two parties with different, or even opposing, interests. When a toddler doesn't eat what is served at mealtime or is restricted from preferring certain foods, this creates challenges and stress for both parent and child.

Why It's Happening

A toddler's need for autonomy is the main driver of their behavior. They may challenge food choices as a way to exercise this autonomy. They might want to do the following:

- Test the limits imposed by their parents
- Explore other eating options
- Let a parent know that they genuinely don't like the food they are given
- Let a parent know that their bodies have a different internal clock for hunger and satiation

What to Do

Make mealtimes a time to connect (STEP 4) through laughter, play, and relaxation. This is more beneficial in the long term than "winning" a food fight.

If the mealtime becomes a battle, your child will inevitably associate food with tension, anxiety, and fear later on in life.

How to Act

1. Stay calm (STEP 1) and embrace the present moment.

2. When you dine out, try to give your child food similar to what they would eat at home or share from your own plate. Avoid ordering from the kids-only menu so they feel equal and included and get a chance to taste a variety of foods.

3. Encourage your toddler to experiment with different tastes and textures and allow them to reject what they don't want to eat without judgment or threats.

4. Praise their curiosity ("I see you tried something new") rather than lauding food-related behavior ("You ate all your banana. You're such a good girl!").

5. Let toddlers eat with their hands. They are naturally curious to discover the world around them through touch and smell—just prepare for the mess!

6. Listen to the cries and tantrums at mealtime with love and affection (STEPS 3 and 4).

Teaching Moment

Does your toddler's challenges with food bring up your own beliefs about eating expectations? If "food fights" become a habit with your toddler, experiment with different mealtimes or schedules and try other options. Then reflect on your own level of relaxation around mealtimes with these questions:

- ▸ What is the cause of my tension and fear around food?
- ▸ What am I afraid of when my toddler refuses to eat?
- ▸ What do I remember about mealtimes and food in my family when I was a child?

TRY THIS INSTEAD

Offer multiple choices of whole, fresh, and nutrient-rich foods every day. Let go of your own self-limiting beliefs and educate yourself about healthy nutrition.

NAPS AND SLEEPING

Some toddlers naturally develop a consistent sleep schedule, while others are up at all hours. Your toddler might nap once or twice a day and fall asleep easily at night, or they might not nap at all and struggle with bedtimes. A fight around naps or bedtime usually happens when a toddler doesn't sleep as expected.

Why It's Happening

A toddler needs between 12 and 14 hours of sleep to grow and develop a healthy mind and body. This need is related to learning and long-term memory in young children.

If your toddler doesn't sleep well, they might be overstimulated by too many activities (or not enough) or too much TV and screen time. They might be afraid of the dark or of having nightmares. Many toddlers simply don't want to miss out on fun activities, such as staying up late, reading, or playing with toys. They would rather exercise their newly discovered independence, and this is in direct conflict with a parent's desire to help their child rest.

What to Do

Each child has their own special internal clock that tells them when their body needs sleep. Watch your toddler for the early clues they use to let you know when they are getting tired.

If your toddler is refusing to lie down for a nap or go to bed, remain calm (STEP 1). A toddler needs your love more than ever when sleep deprived. An overtired or exhausted child cannot think clearly and will probably start to behave irrationally. A child's nervous system needs a lot of cues for connection to calm down in order to fall asleep.

Develop napping and bedtime routines that are consistent and predictable for your toddler.

Add 10 to 15 minutes of physical play, like roughhousing, into your bedtime routine to help your child release tension and to increase connection.

How to Act

1. Follow a regular sleep routine. Start with roughhousing, then cuddling or a bath, or dim the lights for a bedtime story. Whatever works for you.

2. Notice what your toddler is doing. Look for patterns such as hiding in the closet, asking for a snack, or wanting to play a new game. Simply be aware of the behavior without trying to fix it.

3. Set a clear, firm, and loving limit (STEPS 3 and 4). Doing so may trigger a reaction from unresolved emotions such as fear, sadness, or jealousy. Let them cry, stomp, or protest to release these emotions.

4. Tell your child that you are there for them. Say, "I am here with you. You are not alone. I love you so much. You are so precious. Whatever scared you, it is gone now. You are safe."

Teaching Moment

If sleep issues trigger or exhaust you, consider this an invitation for introspection and change. Discover your own needs, anxiety, and fear around sleep time by reflecting on these questions:

- Am I taking good care of myself first? Do I sleep enough?
- Am I asking for help when I feel exhausted?
- Who is helping me with my toddler? If I don't have any help, can I find someone to assist me?
- How was sleep time/bedtime/nighttime for me as a child?
- What is my toddler reminding me of from my own childhood?
- What is one thing that I can do today to help myself feel replenished and supported?

TRY THIS INSTEAD

Prioritize your time for sleep. This is the best way for our mind and body to replenish and revitalize so we can be present for our children when they need us the most.

LEAVING THE HOUSE

While toddlers have a big need for autonomy, they do not perceive time and space as adults do. Toddlers live in the here and now. They enjoy the present moment and have no reason to rush or abide to a schedule that they can't understand. Challenges with going out or leaving the house may appear when doing so interrupts their connection with the present.

Why It's Happening

A toddler does not have a rational understanding of what a schedule is yet. They need time to transition from one activity to something else. And their interest in one activity can be unpredictable and inconsistent. They might spend 30 minutes playing with blocks, and the next day they have no interest in them.

This can be frustrating for parents. There is no predictable foundation for how a day will unfold, yet we still need to do chores, pick up groceries, or go to the bank. Your toddler is curious, and you are a good parent who is probably exhausted.

What to Do

Take a moment to reevaluate and adopt a flexible mindset about your to-do list (STEP 5) so that you can be in the present with yourself and your child. Catch yourself every time you say, "I have to do this/that. I should do this/that." Learn to question the words "have" and "should." In reality, there are very few things we *must* do right now.

How to Act

1. Allow your toddler time to transition from one activity to another.

2. Set a firm and loving limit (**STEP 3**) when needed. For example, say, "I can't let you ride without the seat belt. I will put you in your car seat now."

3. Let your toddler cry, rebel, or protest when confronted with a firm limit. This can actually lead to better cooperation.

4. Listen to your toddler's emotions with compassion, empathy, and love. Validate their feelings with simple and neutral statements. Say, "I see that you feel really angry right now."

5. Trust that when your toddler finishes this healing and emotional work, they will be open to following instruction and better able to collaborate with those around them.

Teaching Moment

Toddlers are spiritual teachers in many ways. Their challenges and conflicts around time teach us to live in the present moment. There is no past or future, only *now*.

If this concept feels difficult to you, reflect on these questions:

- In what areas of my life do I feel most pressured to achieve?
- Was I allowed time to play when I was a child?
- What would happen if I didn't do everything I think I "must" do? What is my biggest fear?

TRY THIS INSTEAD

Your toddler can feel your tension. You can connect with your child only from a place of relaxation and inner awareness.

Start by eliminating "I have to" and "I should" from your language and replace them with "I want to." When you do, you will discover that many of the tasks on your to-do list aren't things that you really want to do but that you force yourself to do at the expense of your authenticity. For example, instead of thinking "I *have* to go to the park with my baby in the morning," say "I *want* to go to the park with my baby in the morning."

How does that feel in your body? If it gives you joy and excitement, then follow this feeling and move toward "accomplishing" this task. If not, then leave it for another time.

SOCIAL EVENTS

Social events are interactions with extended family, neighbors, and members of the larger community beyond the home, including birthday parties, holidays, playdates, and so on.

Why It's Happening

If a child is resistant to social gatherings or events, it is because they do not feel safe and connected. This lack of safety and emotional connection means they are unable to follow rules or meet social expectations.

What to Do

Take a moment to reestablish emotional connection and safety (STEPS 4 and 5).

If you feel caught in the heat of the moment, remember to pause, breathe, and find calm. (A frazzled parent cannot help a child.) Reassess the situation and ensure that your child is safe. Let go of "what needs to happen" and allow their behavior without trying to fix or correct it. Prioritize play and connection instead.

How to Act

1. Introduce some one-on-one play for five minutes. Invite your child by saying: "I'll do anything you want for five minutes."

2. Show enthusiasm. Be fully present and delight in your child's imagination.

3. If you need to set a limit with your toddler, do so with kindness but firmness.

4. Listen to and validate any feelings. Say, "I am here. I see this is hard for you. I love you."

Teaching Moment

A toddler who resists "socially appropriate" behavior is a strong trigger for many parents. We might feel shame as a result of what others might think of us. Turn this awareness inward and use it to question your beliefs about social expectations. Read STEP 1 and reflect on these questions:

- ▸ How do I feel when my toddler displays unpleasant behavior in public?
- ▸ Did I allow my toddler ample time to transition to this new environment?
- ▸ Did I connect with my toddler through play and/or listening before transitioning to this new environment?

TRY THIS INSTEAD

Honor your child's rhythm and preferences without forcing or pressuring them to please others or fit in. Model this behavior by making authentic decisions for yourself first when it comes to social interactions.

ROUTINES AND RITUALS

Routines are predictable daily activities that create a sense of safety and certainty. Rituals are repeatable activities that create a sense of connection between a parent or caregiver and a child.

They are both important because all children—but especially toddlers—thrive on predictability, which teaches a child that they are safe. They learn to rely on the adults around them to be present, caring, and available and to be a source of love and connection. Through routines, a child learns to trust the predictable moments in a day and to develop a sense of certainty in relationship to their environment. During the toddler years, most routines revolve around eating, playing, and sleeping.

In this chapter, you'll learn some routines and rituals that you can use to create connection with your toddler. While there are common rituals that revolve around certain themes or events, they can also be personal and unique to every family.

MORNINGS

If your toddler has settled into a nightly sleep schedule, you may be able to anticipate when they will wake and create a morning routine around that time. After breakfast, initiate a routine of **Morning Play.**

Schedule 30 to 60 minutes (or however long you can) of play to give your toddler an opportunity to connect with you. This could be reading together, playing with a special toy, going for a walk outside, or running around in the backyard. Follow your toddler's lead, rather than trying to control or direct, and strive for a balance between child-led play and unstructured (free) play, both inside the home and outside. Allow plenty of room for silence and self-discovery in between interactions.

Rituals for Connection

START THE MORNING WITH A HUG. When your toddler wakes, make hugging an intentional act. Be present in the hug for one long minute and receive with gratitude the new day as a gift to you to spend with your child. Try the following:

> *"Good morning, my love! I am so happy to see you and be with you today. I want to give you a hug. May I?"* Open your arms wide. *"Look at the sun outside. It's a new day. I love you and I love today."*

Though your toddler can't fully understand the meaning of the words, the energy behind them will express your emotional connection.

SAY A GRATITUDE MANTRA. In the morning, after waking or before leaving the house, repeat a gratitude mantra to your child. This reminds us as a parent to be thankful for each day and models positive behavior for our child. Here's an example that I use with my son:

> *"Thank you for my wonderful life and my wonderful self and my wonderful mom and dad. Thank you for all the love that I feel in my heart. I love you,* [each of you say your own first name]. *I am perfect just the way I am."*

MEALTIMES

Mealtimes offer a beneficial opportunity for togetherness and connection. Settling into a daily schedule that keeps mealtimes fairly constant gives a toddler a sense of expectation, anticipation, and reliability while preparing them for social interactions.

EATING TOGETHER as a family, whenever possible, creates a reliable routine for long-lasting connection. For many working parents, however, this can be a challenge. To treat mealtime routines with reverence and presence, choose one daily meal that you will share together as a family. Consider when everyone in your household is home at the same time and how much time you have to spend together. If you feel exhausted or unprepared to build this routine around dinnertime, explore cooking meals in advance to eat later.

THE 10 MEALTIME COMMANDMENTS

Be mindful of what you say and do in the presence of a toddler. Young children absorb your words and can be affected by the mealtime environment. Here are a few rules of thumb:

1. When possible, feed your child the same meal that you eat.

2. Give your child two or three different foods or healthy snacks to choose from.

3. Even if your child does not eat at this moment, trust that they will not stay hungry.

4. Avoid keeping cell phones or electronic devices on the table during mealtimes.

5. Never argue at the table. Move the discussion elsewhere at another time.

6. Put off making any important, life-changing decisions during mealtimes.

7. Forgo praising your child for how much they eat.

8. Avoid shaming or making your child feel guilty for not eating or eating too little.

9. Sweets or desserts should not be a conditional reward for eating "all the food first."

10. Avoid food-related punishments such as withholding sweets or taking away toys.

Rituals for Connection

Once you've established which mealtime works best for your routine, consider adding a ritual to help signal that it has begun.

SAY GRACE OR A GRATITUDE MANTRA. Before the meal begins, take a short pause to be grateful for all that you have and for one another. This can be spoken aloud or can be silent; it does not have to be religious in nature or expression. You can hold hands as a family or simply say "thank you" to each member seated at the table.

PLAN A WEEKLY PICNIC. Pick one day of the week (for example, every Friday afternoon) and plan a picnic at the park or anywhere outdoors where you can connect with nature. If the weather prohibits going outside, have a picnic indoors, either on the living room floor, in a tent, or under a fort.

DECORATE THE TABLE. Once a month, choose a different theme for the table where you eat your meals and decorate the table according to that theme. Let your toddler help choose the theme of the month. Be accepting and enthusiastic about whatever they decide on.

BATH TIME

Giving your toddler a bath before getting ready to go to bed (and at the same time each evening) is a great way for parents to connect with their child at the end of the day. **Bath Time** can also be part of a soothing bedtime routine, a way to calm your excited toddler and prepare them for story time and sleeping. If there are two parents or caregivers in the home and each is available in the evenings, then agree to take turns giving your child a bath every other night.

Rituals for Connection

BATH TIME FRIENDS. Let your child choose a favorite waterproof toy to join them in the bath each evening.

BUBBLES! Once a week, plan a bubble bath together using a nonirritant solution. Blow bubbles and splash around!

PICK THE PJS. Keep a set of two different pajamas in a dry spot near the bathing area. When your child is done with their bath, let them pick which pajama set to wear to sleep.

SING A SONG. Make up a short bath-time song that you can sing together at the end of the bath.

BEDTIME

There is something magical about helping a toddler unwind after a long day of discoveries and experimentation, successes and failures, and, on some days, emotional turmoil.

Establishing a bedtime routine is very dear to most parents. After dinner, spend 10 to 15 minutes of child-led **Physical Play**. This connecting experience allows a young child to laugh and release any leftover tension accumulated in the day. This play time can then be followed by **Story Time**.

Rituals for Connection

STORY TIME. Ask them to choose a special book from your "I love you" collection. This can be a set of two to five books that reinforce the loving connection you share with your child and how special they are to you. Play soft music while you read aloud or together.

SEND LOVE AND/OR FORGIVENESS. Together, think of three people in the world and send them love wherever they are. This ritual teaches your toddler that love is energy that can travel anywhere in time and space; it has no boundaries. Then, think of three people in the world and send them your forgiveness, which teaches your toddler that forgiveness is also energy that can travel anywhere.

SAY GOOD NIGHT. After story time, when your child is in bed, help them say good night to the things and people they care about. Say "good night" together to their favorite toys and stuffed animals. Look outside and say good night to the moon and stars. Have them close their eyes and put their hand on their heart and say good night to everyone in your family, whether near or far.

WELCOMING

After a long day of separation, the moment of reuniting with our child deserves special acknowledgment. Perhaps you're coming home from work or picking up your child up from daycare. We may feel conflicting feelings, such as joy and guilt, excitement, or helplessness.

A **Welcome Routine** is a moment for us to pause, take a few breaths, detach from the outside world of work and conflict, and reconnect with the world inside ourselves. By doing this, we can greet our child with joy, curiosity, humility, reverence, and gratitude. In response, your child will feel your joy, absorb your positive energy, and connect with your love.

Rituals for Connection

WELCOME HUG. Open your arms wide and hug your child. Allow your toddler to rest in your arms for as long as they need. Then, make eye contact, smile, and say, "I missed you today. I am so happy to hold you in my arms again." Be comfortable with silence until your toddler speaks.

SPEND TIME TOGETHER. Go for a short walk or play together one-on-one, even if it's just for five minutes. Then transition into a dinner or bedtime routine.

SHARE A SECRET HANDSHAKE. Create a special "welcome" handshake or physical signal that's a form of greeting just between you two. This could be a special high five, patty-cake, or fist bump that invites a playful tone to your return.

CHORES

Though toddlers may be too young to do any chores around the house, a parent can model routines around cleaning up, putting away toys, and sorting out clothes or books. In order to build good habits as they grow older, invite your toddler to be your "Generous Helper" with safe chores that they can handle, such as putting toys away before dinner, placing dirty laundry in the washing machine or hamper, putting their books back on a reachable shelf, or handing you groceries to be put away.

Rituals for Connection

THANK YOU. Build a ritual around thanking the books for their stories before putting them back on the shelf. Thank the toys for "playing with us" before putting them away.

SING A SONG. Make up a generous helper song or sing a favorite movie tune together before or after the work is done.

BIRTHDAYS

Birthday celebrations and parties can trigger lots of big feelings for a toddler. They might feel jealous or throw a tantrum. They might want to open the gifts on someone else's birthday, while on their own birthday, your toddler might expect to open their presents right then and there. (**STEPS 3** and **4** can help your toddler in these difficult moments.)

Build a routine around birthday celebrations that reflect gratitude and establish emotional connections and a feeling of safety. If you and your toddler are going to another child's birthday celebration, spend 5 to 10 minutes of undivided one-on-one time with your toddler before going to the party. This will give your toddler a stable emotional connection in case of a tantrum or meltdown.

Rituals for Connection

When celebrating a birthday, incorporate one of the rituals for connection to introduce a moment of gratitude for others.

CREATE A BIRTHDAY CARD. Use finger paints to help your toddler decorate or color a birthday card for a celebrated friend or family member.

MAKE A THANK-YOU CARD. Use finger paints to help your toddler decorate or color a thank-you card for the friends or family members who gave them presents. Let your toddler drop the thank-you cards into a mailbox one by one.

PICK OUT THE PRESENT. Keep a "give-away box" of potential gifts and let your toddler choose an object from the box to wrap and give as a present.

TIMES OF STRESS

Times of stress can be very reactive for a toddler. These moments might be life-changing, such as moving to a new house or school, welcoming a new baby to the family, or losing a family member. Or they might be small moments, such as a barking dog, the sudden clap of thunder, or a new teacher.

During times of stress, change, and crisis, your toddler may react by crying, stomping, or becoming aggressive or uncooperative, and may be unable to follow routines and instructions. These coping mechanisms are a toddler's way of releasing stress. Your toddler needs reassurance that they are safe and loved.

You can build a "stress routine" for moments of crisis so that you are not caught unprepared and risk becoming reactive yourself. Create a **Safe Place** in the home where you and your toddler can rest together when things feel too much, such as a corner in a room, a comfortable armchair, a special couch, a rocking chair, or even laying down on the floor.

Rituals for Connection

HOLD HANDS. Create a ritual so that your toddler knows they are going to the safe place. Hold hands and say "I love you" three times when entering the safe place.

GIVE A HUG. At the end of your time together in the safe place, hug your child and say, "I love you" three times before leaving the safe place.

CONFLICT

Conflicts are very upsetting and disorienting. Whenever your child witnesses conflict or is engaged in it, their feeling of safety is replaced with a feeling of fear and survival. They may question their place in the world and whether or not they are loved.

While conflict should never be a "routine," it is helpful to have a routine to reestablish safety and emotional connection with your child during or after a conflict.

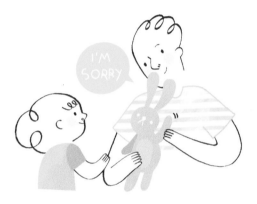

You can use this routine in the following scenarios:

- You or a partner yell in front of your child. Say, "It's not your fault that we yelled at each other today. I am sorry we scared you. We both love you very much."
- You yell at your child. Say, "It's not your fault that I lost my temper with you earlier. I am sorry I yelled at you. I love you very much."
- Experiencing difficulties while co-parenting. Say, "It's not your fault that you didn't want to come with me today, after your time with [Mom or Dad]. I am sorry I couldn't let you stay longer. We both love you very much."

- Conflict around sharing. Say, "It wasn't your fault that you didn't want to share your toy with your friend. I am sorry I couldn't support both of you better. I love you very much."

Rituals for Connection

PLAY A GAME. Let your toddler choose a game for you to play together once the conflict has ended.

SAY "I'M SORRY." Pick up one of your toddler's stuffed toys or animals and mime with it saying "I am sorry. Please forgive me. I love you."

QUIET TIME TOGETHER. Spend time together painting or drawing or sharing a creative craft. Play soft music in the background. If home was the place of conflict, go for a long walk.

PORTABLE ROUTINES

We travel with our toddlers regularly, whether it's going on vacations, visiting relatives and friends, driving around town on errands, or walking to the neighborhood park.

Young children need time to transition from one activity to another and they need familiarity with their environment to feel safe. Children feel scared and helpless when taken by surprise, such as when a parent disappears to travel for work or the family packs for a "sudden" vacation.

Build a portable routine that announces **What's Next** so your toddler knows what's to come.

For example, if you're planning a long trip, give your toddler time to prepare and get used to the idea. Take your toddler's suitcase or backpack out one to two weeks before the trip. Keep it in their room or a play area and leave it wide open. Let them start "packing" their three favorite toys and five sets of clothes for the trip. Show your curiosity about what they are packing and be supportive. Let them get used to the idea that a longer trip is coming and to experiment with what to pack. This kind of routine around traveling is fun and builds trust.

Rituals for Connection

PLAY FAVORITES. Help your toddler pack a beloved toy, book, or item of clothing for the trip.

PROTECTION MANTRA. Say a protection prayer or mantra before you leave the house to go on the trip: "*Please surround me and my family with the light of protection, here and now, and wherever we will be traveling. I thank you for infinite protection.*"

COLLECT MEMORIES. Help your child keep a special travel journal that they can draw or paint in to remember their experience. You can also print a photo album after the trip and keep it in your home.

CREATING BONDING TRADITIONS WITH YOUR TODDLER

These routines suggest a way to reserve a special time between you and your toddler; to show love, resolve issues, and reinforce emotional connection. Rituals can serve to teach young children how to practice gratitude, compassion, forgiveness, and generosity; to engage their imagination and creativity; and to provide a moment of stillness amid chaos. As your toddler grows up into a child and then, eventually, an adult with children of their own, these routines and rituals will stay with them, passing on the tradition of love and emotional connection for generations.

RESOURCES

ON THE WEB

Aha! Parenting: ahaparenting.com

Attachment Parenting: attachmentparenting.org

Authentic Parenting: naomialdort.com

Aware Parenting: awareparenting.com

Parenting by Connection: handinhandparenting.org

Positive Parenting: positivediscipline.com

BOOKS

Aldort, Naomi, PhD. *Raising Our Children, Raising Ourselves: Transforming Parent-Child Relationships from Reaction and Struggle to Freedom, Power and Joy*. Bothell, WA: Book Publishers Network, 2015.

Cohen, Lawrence J., PhD. *Playful Parenting: An Exciting New Approach to Raising Children That Will Help You Nurture Close Connections, Solve Behavior Problems, and Encourage Confidence*. New York: Ballantine Books, 2001.

DeBenedet, Anthony T., and Lawrence J. Cohen, PhD. *The Art of Roughhousing: Good Old-Fashioned Horseplay and Why Every Kid Needs It*. Philadelphia: Quirk Books, 2010.

Markham, Laura, PhD. *Peaceful Parent, Happy Kids: How to Stop Yelling and Start Connecting*. New York: Perigree, 2012.

Siegel, Daniel, PhD, and Mary Hartzell. *Parenting from the Inside Out: How a Deeper Self-Understanding Can Help You Raise Children Who Thrive*. New York: Penguin, 2014.

Tsabary, Shefali, PhD. *The Conscious Parent: Transforming Ourselves, Empowering Our Children*. Vancouver, Canada: Namaste Publishing, 2010.

Wipfler, Patty, and Tosha Shore, MA. *Listen: Five Simple Tools to Meet Your Everyday Parenting Challenges*. Palo Alto, CA: Hand in Hand Parenting, 2016.

INDEX

ACKNOWLEDGMENTS

My editor, Sabrina Young. Thank you for making this book so much more beautiful. Thank you for your gift and patience with me.

Sandro Formica. Thank you for bringing me closer to my own consciousness and inner potentiality. I am beyond grateful.

My spiritual coach, Codruta Muntean. Thank you for helping me find my light in the dark. I am forever grateful.

Patty Wipfler, founder of Hand in Hand Parenting and a visionary in the field of parenting education.

Kirsten Nottleson, my exquisite mentor.

My parents, Cornelia and Ion, and my siblings, Marina and Ovidiu. Thank you for your love.

My high school teachers and classmates. Thank you for giving me the foundation to become who I am today.

My mentors at Florida International University. Thank you for trusting me to be myself and grow as a leader and teacher.

My close friends. Thank you for being there for me unconditionally. I love you with all my heart.

ABOUT THE AUTHOR

Mihaela Plugarasu, MS, is an educator with more than 15 years of leadership, self-development, and teaching experience. She is a mom, co-parent, and college professor in Miami, Florida, who lectures in the United States, Europe, and Latin America.

She became intentional about conscious parenting ever since her son was born and her life changed profoundly as a result of looking within. Mihaela is the first certified parent educator for parenting-by-connection in Florida, by Hand in Hand Parenting. In this role, she facilitates parent support groups, workshops, classes, and individual work with families.

Mihaela is the founder of parentingmadeconscious.com, a community of conscious parents who come together for the purpose of learning, personal evolution, and creating a connection-based relationship with their children.